CHILDREN
OF EXILE

CHILDREN
OF EXILE

ADRIAN SNELL
WITH JENNY ROBERTSON

WORD PUBLISHING

WORD (UK) Ltd
Milton Keynes, England

WORD AUSTRALIA
Kilsyth, Victoria, Australia

WORD COMMUNICATIONS LTD
Vancouver, B.C., Canada

STRUIK CHRISTIAN BOOKS (PTY) LTD
Maitland, South Africa

ALBY COMMERCIAL ENTERPRISES PTE LTD
Balmoral Road, Singapore

CHRISTIAN MARKETING NEW ZEALAND LTD
Havelock North, New Zealand

JENSCO LTD
Hong Kong

SALVATION BOOK CENTRE
Malaysia

CHILDREN OF EXILE

ISBN 0-85009-236-1 (paper) 0-85009-249-3 (cased)
Australia ISBN 1-86258-130-4 (paper) ISBN 1-86258-160-6 (cased)

Unless otherwise stated, all biblical quotations are from the Holy Bible, New International Version, © 1973, 1978, 1984 by the International Bible Society.

Pp.56-57: Excerpt from the Foreword by François Mauriac from *Night* by Elie Wiesel, originally published in French by Les Éditions de Minuit, 1958. English translation copyright © 1960 by MacGibbon and Kee. Reprinted by permission of Hill and Wang, a division of Farrar, Straus and Giroux, Inc.

On pp.18 and 100 extracts from *God's Beloved* (author unknown) and on pp.44, 84, and 89 extracts from *If I Were* by Israel Najara are from *The Penguin Book of Hebrew Verse*, translated by T. Carmi (Allen Lane, 1981), copyright © T. Carmi, 1981 and reproduced by permission of Penguin Books Ltd. (Adrian Snell has adapted these poems in order to set them to music.)

On pp.27 and 94 extracts from *The Song of an Exile (Shir Golah)* by Menahem Mendel Dolitzki are from *A History of Jewish Literature* (volume 4) by Waxman (New York: Block Publishing Co. 1941), reproduced by permission.

On p.49 *Fear* by Eva Picková and on pp.53-55 *Terezín* by Hanŭs Hachenburg are from *I Never Saw Another Butterfly*, reproduced by permission of the State Jewish Museum, Prague.

Songs from ALPHA AND OMEGA, copyright © 1986 (Adrian Snell/Phil Thomson) Word Music (UK).

Songs from FATHER copyright © 1990 Word Music (UK), except for *Goodbye October* (Adrian Snell/Phil Thomson) copyright © 1976 Thankyou Music.

On p.61 *Only Jesus* (Adrian Snell/Barry Crompton) and p.102 *Take Me Home* copyright © 1984 Word Music (UK).

Illustrations on pp.8,10,25,34,44,63 and 73 by James Kessell.

Typesetting by Phoenix Manor, Milton Keynes.
Reproduced, printed and bound in Great Britain for Word (UK) by Richard Clay Ltd., Bungay.

91 92 93 94 / 10 9 8 7 6 5 4 3 2 1

To Susan

Acknowledgements

Very special thanks to Jenny Robertson for sharing this journey with me; to Win Kennedy and Susan Snell for their work on the editing of the manuscript; to Aad and Jeanette Vermeyden for endless research and valued friendship; to Noël Halsey for continuing encouragement at each stage; and to so many friends and associates, some mentioned in this book, others not, who are a part of this story, often in ways they cannot fully know.

Contents

Foreword

Ever since Adam and Eve were driven out of the Garden of Eden, in one way or another exile has been part of the human experience. Most often it was, and continues to be into our own days, a physical uprooting. Indeed, it is my firm conviction that when future historians come to give their verdict on our century, they will characterise it not only as the one which witnessed the two most destructive world wars in history — but as the century of the refugees. If we drew even faint pencil marks on a globe of our world, they would very soon darken its continents and oceans with lines of men, women and children moving from places where they are not wanted to new countries and societies which are so often reluctant to welcome them.

There are also people who become internal exiles. The spiritual world we inhabit is likewise dotted with ideals betrayed and failed ideologies. Perhaps the oldest sin is idolatry, the worship and service of power which takes on an almost endless variety of guises, the things that our clever hands and minds can get us, the possessions we hold so dear that we do not even notice the point at which they begin to possess us. I am equally convinced that it is only genuine religious faith which can rescue and save from the fashionable temptations of the day.

Yet the one who is in exile is not so much lost as on a journey. It is a journey which can deepen the moral strain in men and women and can transform an entire people. To be an outsider is to be in a hard school of life, and yet ..... there can be purification through suffering. Those who experience pain themselves can have great sympathy for the vulnerable and the miserable. Those who taste the bitter cup of loneliness and abandonment can have the opportunity to discover that love of God and love of neighbour go hand in hand.

I think of the Children of Israel and the exodus from the slavery and degradation of Egypt, of their life-renewing halt at the foothills of Sinai and the move towards the Promised Land. I picture the exiles weeping by the waters of Babylon but soon, as if driven by the far greater force of life, building houses, living decent lives in them and, as the prophet Jeremiah advised them, praying for the welfare of their new city and working hard to make it a bastion of civilisation.

Among those who make ongoing life possible, place of honour must be given to the poets and the singers who can give permanent value to that which was left behind, who can comfort and console, and who can inspire with hope in the future.

Adrian Snell is one of those special souls whose personality is defined by his religious faith and his music. He is a searcher, embarked on a lifelong pilgrimage in quest of spiritual truths.

It may have been no more than a professional engagement that took him to the region of Bergen-Belsen in Germany, but there imagination and sensitivity took over and transformed the experience into one of deepest understanding and sharing something of the agony which has permeated the very soil and air in that Godforsaken place. So it was when he entered the pain in a leper colony in India and when he strolled with his terminally ill father. I single out these episodes from the many recounted in this book because I am a survivor of Nazi concentration camps myself, served as a rabbi in India for three years and came to know a little of the glory as well as the pain in that remarkable country, and because — by purest coincidence — I also knew and admired Adrian's father when he was Bishop of Croydon. I am moved too by Adrian's discovery and his conviction that God is more to be found in darkness and ugliness than in the saccharine-sweet stereotypes that so often pass for religion.

In the pages that follow much is made of a remarkable Jewish prayer, called the *Kaddish*. Originally an Aramaic doxology or hymn of praise about God's creative holiness, which the rabbis of two thousand years ago recited when they concluded their studies, it soon became associated with mourning the death of one's nearest and dearest. It is derived from the Semitic root-word *KDSH* which means 'holy' — a key concept in Judaism, Christianity and Islam, the three traditions of religious faith that began with Abraham.

The call to men and women of flesh and blood in the Book of Leviticus: "Be holy, for I the Lord your God am holy!" (19:1) is one of the most revolutionary calls in the spiritual life of humanity. It insists that even the most sublime of divine attributes can be imitated by human beings. In Judaism this led to what I often describe as 'a spiritual technique'. Ordinary things and everyday events can be filled with an ideal or a set of ideals and in that way lifted to the level of holiness. Ordinary time, when it is devoted to rest, family, prayer with the community and personal reflection, becomes 'the holy Sabbath'. The Hebrew term for marriage is *Kiddushin*, a special relationship of love and the union of complementary personalities. For Jews, Jerusalem is the *ir hakodesh*, 'the holy city' because one of its modest hills, Mount Zion, is a code-word for the place where it will be clear to everyone when God's Kingdom on earth will be established by a redeemed humanity, fully grown people conscious of their partnership with God. Even a powerful memory that speaks of life and love shared is holy — hence the *Kaddish*.

I commend to you, dear reader, Adrian Snell's instinctive discovery of this truth. In the many countries he visited and the audiences he encountered sparks of holiness light up the way. *Kaddish* is as much his tribute to the memory of children who composed such poignant poems in their prison in Terezín, before their exile was so heartlessly ended in the gas-chambers of Auschwitz, as it is to the memory of the father he knew and loved.

Physical or emotional exile is the experience of many of us, but those who have an awareness that they are under the sheltering wing of the Divine Presence are never abandoned. As I was reading Adrian's story and reflecting on the texts of his songs, I found myself humming a song taught to me such a long time ago that I am not even certain by whom. Perhaps it was my father — or my grandfather. At one time or another I sang it with both of them. *Du* is a Yiddish word which means 'You!' and its title is simply *A Dudele* — 'a little You song'. It was written about two hundred years ago by Levi Yizchak of Berdichev — and I have the feeling that he and Adrian Snell would have understood each other perfectly.

Where I wander — You!
Where I ponder — You!
Only You, You again, always You!
You! You! You!
When I am gladdened — You!
When I am saddened — You!
Only You, You again, always You!
You! You! You!
Sky is You, earth is You!
You above! You below!
In every trend, at every end,
Only You, You again, always You!
You! You! You!

Rabbi Hugo Gryn

Chapter One

The earth will reveal ..... her slain

Music is my language. Artists use colour on canvas, but I describe in sound. I've been learning the language of music ever since I was small. I started playing the piano when I was six, and even then I made up my own tunes. Of course, it was no more than the sort of cacophony all small children make — for I was learning not just to make a sound, but to listen to what that sound said.

Music expresses joy and sorrow. It dances. It marches. It sings along with whatever we're doing at the moment. It reaches for the eternal. But for me, above all, music is the language of the heart. I express my emotion in musical form. And so music is the most natural and most fulfilling way of sharing something I hold very dear: my Christian faith.

Music creates a response not only of the mind, but of the spirit and the heart. It reaches the part of us we still call our soul. I think most people agree that the tired concept of mind over matter has led us to a desperate place. Now more than ever before we realise we must learn to listen to what our heart says. Music not only helps us listen. It takes us into a new understanding. Over the last few years my music has taken me along a path of pain which I am still exploring. It has taken me into darkness. It's not too much to say that I have heard the very earth weep.

I want to share my journey with you. Come with me and my music along a path which will go back into my childhood and forward through albums and concept works which have taken me to places of pain and sorrow, to cities which have been at the forefront of mind-shattering events, to a city whose very name means peace. There will be struggle, but there will be joy and, beyond that, a song in which all the music of the earth is just the faintest echo: a song in which all music ends.

*   *   *

We'll start in March, 1985 in a truck full of equipment speeding along an autobahn with me and three Dutch colleagues. We're on our way to give a concert in a British army base somewhere in north-west Germany.

The actual place wasn't our main concern. Getting to the base, getting set up and playing the selection of songs we'd chosen was what we had to concentrate on. I stared into the night ahead and wished my wife Sue were with me.

I owe so much to Sue: the support she gives me in this work, her willingness to hold our home and our three children together when I'm touring, the practical ways she lives out the faith we share together, which holds us all.

The next day, after the concert, after the experience which shook me and started me on my pilgrimage, I wished even more that Sue was with me. Simply to walk where I was walking. Simply to share. To hear not music but tears. Tears and blood. The eternal sadness which I was going to turn into music.

But I knew nothing of that as the truck pulled into the army camp.

Knew nothing — yet felt an immediate sense of unease. An oppression.

Perhaps it was the barbed wire, the official notices, the sense that an army means an enemy. The country we were in was divided. Back in 1985 the Cold War was still an icy reality. There were no cracks in the ice. The Iron Curtain cloaked the Soviet Union and its satellites in secrecy. Only months before our concert the forces of terror had shocked the world with the murder of the Polish Solidarity priest, Father Jerzy Popieluszko.

The British Army to whom I had come as guest could well point to this latest violation of human rights to justify their presence in Federal Germany.

The chaplain met us, and we got ready for the concert. As we were unloading our equipment all sorts of things went wrong, sharpening our sense of unease, heightening the tension. Then it was time to go on. I looked out over the lights. I felt that familiar race of adrenalin. That familiar sense of thrill — how generous people are, coming along on

The camp Belsen, the morning after liberation
Feliks Topolski © National Museum, Warsaw, used with permission.

a cold March night to share my music, to share, I pray, my Lord.

There was some heckling, but we moved on through a selection of songs from *THE PASSION*. Then there was a breakdown of equipment.

That's a bad feeling. The artist carries on, but everyone feels bad.

Yet it was more than a technical hitch. My heart was heavy. There's a spiritual battle happening here, I thought.

Afterwards the chaplain and I got into conversation. "I'm sorry about the heckling," he apologised. "But apart from that how do you feel about the way things went?"

"On the whole the audience were encouraging," I began, but then I came right out with it and told him how I was feeling. "I've never felt so much oppression."

He looked at me.

"You didn't realise then? This camp is situated two kilometres from the site of the Bergen-Belsen concentration camp."

Bergen-Belsen! Of course I had heard of the notorious Nazi death camp. But was this enough to explain the awful sense of oppression we'd all been feeling since our arrival here, the sense too of spiritual warfare?

"Look out there," the chaplain continued. "There's a patch of grass. It may be a mass grave. No one knows for sure. And over there — that was once the SS Headquarters."

So here, in the middle of what is generally viewed as a peace-keeping army base, the mass murderers of the last war plotted death. As I absorbed that fact, I felt I was taking into myself an oppressive weight, and I wasn't surprised when the chaplain told me that there's a high incidence of breakdown among the personnel in that base. As he cited examples, I sensed that people here who broke down, for whatever external reason, were also making an appropriate response. They could no longer separate their deepest self from a pain many of us are blind to.

And neither could I.

Brokenness is probably the only true response. Brokenness and then personal involvement. The mending of minds, the building of trust between people, the healing of the fractured

earth itself depend upon our response. I was to learn that
the next day. It was the start of a journey for me, and the
rest of this book, the rest of my music so far flows from it.

And I knew without any shadow of doubt that I would
have to make that journey. For a start I would travel those
two kilometres the chaplain had talked about, visit Bergen-
Belsen and absorb whatever it would say to me.

The following day I set off for the camp with my Dutch
colleagues.

We talked as we went.

"How did you sleep?"

"Fine, only I woke up to a strange kind of sensation.
Vibrations. As though the earth was trembling."

"I felt it too," I said. "I asked an officer what it was. He
said we were experiencing a NATO exercise. Those
vibrations come from explosions."

We reflected on this and went on in silence, while guns
exploded in mock warfare and the ground beneath us shook.

We entered a place of silence. You pass through the gates
and then there is only silence. Silence and stones. Stone
after stone marks the mass graves where bodies were
thrown. Each stone bears a number: 500. 1000. Stone after
stone.

The ground still shook with vibrations. Cannon fire
punctuated our steps. And it seemed to me I heard a voice
cry out in pain. Did the earth cry? Or was it the voice of
God?

My children lie here, my murdered ones, and cannot rest
for the noise of guns. O earth, earth give voice, for the blood
of my children screams from the ground, and you do not
hear above the loud sound of guns.

The day was grey and damp. Rain started to fall. Even the
sky was weeping. And still the guns rumbled, shaking the
ground which covered thirty thousand dead.

I sensed the broken heart of God as never before. "Here,"
I felt God say, "where thirty thousand of my children lie
buried, there is no peace on the earth because still you
rehearse for war."

Then I knew I would have to describe in music the sound
of those guns, the eternal sadness I sensed around me, the

Bergen-Belsen
© Yad Vashem, Jerusalem, used with permission.

Memorial stone at Bergen-Belsen
© Yad Vashem, Jerusalem, used with permission.

lingering sorrow of this place and the righteous anger of God at the murder of His children.

One day God will roll back the ground of Europe and reveal the true story of centuries of warfare. There are forest glades in the heart of Europe where, amidst trees burgeoning with spring, men, women and children were forced to undress and queue up to be shot. Soldiers snatched babies from their mothers' arms and threw them into the grave first. And still the birds sang in the trees. Nest building went on. Branches swayed with life. The sun still shone.

And now we pollute the planet, destroying the very web of our existence. We have anaesthetised even the concept of justice. We forget that Abel's blood cried out from the ground and God heard that cry and condemned Cain for his brother's murder.

"Am I my brother's keeper?" Cain asked his God.

The terror of the SS took place because the world refused to bear responsibility. Similarly, the rape of our planet continues because we are learning too late to bear responsibility for the very earth which nurtures and sustains us.

This is a sombre truth, but the survival of our race depends upon our realising it.

There is a new stone in Bergen-Belsen now. President Chaim Herzog of Israel unveiled it in 1987, during a momentous visit to Federal Germany. The stone bears a verse from the Psalms written in German and Hebrew which reads: "My sorrow is continually before me."

These prophetic words lead to psychic and global health. Only when we listen to the voice of sorrow can we ever learn to hear one another. Our shared weeping leads to real trust: the trust which heals the nations. And when we hear the sorrow of the earth we understand the extent of its pollution, and long for the cleansing the Messiah will bring.

Back in the eighth century BC the prophet Isaiah wrote words which have become so meaningful to me after that visit to Bergen-Belsen, that I made them the basis of a new musical work, *ALPHA AND OMEGA*.

Your dead will live;
their bodies will rise.
You who dwell in the dust,
wake up and shout for joy.
Your dew is like the dew of the morning;
the earth will give birth to her dead .....
See, the Lord is coming out of his dwelling
to punish the people of the earth for their sins.
The earth will disclose the blood shed upon her;
she will conceal her slain no longer.

(Isaiah 26: 19 and 21 NIV)

ALPHA AND OMEGA begins with the sounds of war
which lie at the heart of the lyric *Guns of Peace*. It has led me
into the music of *SONG OF AN EXILE*, and from there to my
later album *FATHER*. At the centre of all these works is the
embrace of love and the joy which comes when we find
ourselves part of a healed relationship. The music of pain is
the music of reconciliation.

And I must share with you now that the people who have
been able to receive the message of this music are those who
are aware of their own failure, who listen from a background
of brokenness which contains neither arrogance nor
triumphalism.

This is a music which has led me to many exciting new
friendships. It has taken me on a journey of the heart, and
on a physical journey. After that visit to Bergen-Belsen in
March 1985, I returned home with my mind full of new
music to discover that the next landmark on this journey
would be Jerusalem itself, the "City of Peace".

Chapter Two

City of peace

About two months before that visit to Bergen-Belsen in March 1985, I had been on a concert tour of Norway which left me with no doubt in my mind that I had to work on a new project. I knew that my music needed new direction. In addition, I was feeling increasingly uncomfortable with the whole machinery of Christian concerts. I say this as someone who is very much part of this work, but the people who are most involved are the ones who have the greatest right to think critically about what they do. That was one of the things I learnt from my father. He was a bishop in the Church of England. He listened to my juvenile rumblings about formalism and traditionalism. My faith had taken me in far more radical directions than cloisters and choir boys in ruffs. Dad accepted my comments, but then he would say: "The Church is like a family. You can grouse and moan but you still belong, warts and all!"

That piece of fatherly wisdom took some of the heat off my attack, though I felt some of the old discontent later in 1988, when we took *ALPHA AND OMEGA* on a tour of English cathedrals and I had a bit of relearning to do. Growing up, you could call it. Learning grace. Even working with choirs required some rethinking on my part. But that was still in the future. All I knew at the beginning of 1985 was that I was changing and so was my music. The visit to Bergen-Belsen took me further along that road. In fact, it changed the whole direction of my music.

ALPHA AND OMEGA is a proclamation of hope. I was drawn to the splendid vision of Jerusalem as the City of God, the City of Peace, the city of new beginnings for us all. All this is expressed in the song *Alpha and Omega*: "rejoice, the Holy City comes". It is a song of joy, and for many people it perfectly expresses our wonderful hope: that we shall see our God face to face. But for me now, the whole work had become one of brokenness and sorrow, and even the triumphant pieces are born out of pain: the pain of a loving God who longs to hold us, bloodstained as we are, safe in His embrace, as expressed in the song *Child of Darkness*:

Born to love Me, pure in My eyes
Oh, My child, I held you close to My side
And with a Father's loving care
I made a world for you and I to share.

Child of darkness, blind to My light
You have turned against Me into the night
How long will you remain untrue?
Far from the shelter of My wing
So far from the love I long to bring to you.

Come oh children hear what I say
For My heart is open if you obey
All that is Mine I freely give
Yet if you turn and spurn My love
My sword shall fall, you shall not live in Me.

Child of sorrow, living in fear
If you call upon Me I shall be near
Come, let us reason, you will see
Crimson that flows till white as snow
For though you have sinned
My love will set you free.

This music, this message of love and reconciliation pulsed inside me. Then, within two weeks of my return from Bergen-Belsen, I received a letter from Dr. Clifford Hill, sociologist and theologian, author of *Towards the Dawn* and *The Day Comes*. *The Day Comes* had already made a tremendous impression on me. Now he was writing to me about an international conference to be held in Jerusalem the following year. The conference would involve Christians from an incredible range of countries: from China, Uganda, the Eastern bloc, as it was known then, as well as the West.

So here was I, burning with conviction, longing for a new direction and here was a letter about a conference for men and women with a recognised prophetic ministry in their own country to gather in Jerusalem the week before Easter, to shoulder together the cross of worldwide need, to pray and return home with new vision. That was exciting enough, but now came a request which confirmed absolutely everything I was feeling in my deepest being.

Would I write a work which would be performed at the end of that conference?

Music, as a response to everything which Bergen-Belsen had awoken within me, was taking shape in my mind. I was ready to write, and in autumn 1985 I began work with poet and lyricist Phil Thomson on *ALPHA AND OMEGA*. We had worked together before, and now we wanted to express the impact of those sounds of war which had shaken the graves of thousands of unnamed dead.

With all this in our hearts, Phil and I went off to see Clifford Hill and discussed the whole project with him. Clifford too was wrestling with the great themes of Isaiah. Our thoughts were completely in tune.

And now begins another strand in my story — one, however, which is linked to the very name Israel, "the one who struggles". For we would all struggle with the new concept of *ALPHA AND OMEGA*, with the best way in which to present it. And there were to be many, many struggles of various kinds in bringing *ALPHA AND OMEGA* and *SONG OF AN EXILE* to our audiences. Each one of us most intimately involved would feel it: struggles to understand the thinking behind these works; struggles to even begin to embrace the enormity of the Holocaust, of the rape of the earth, of world hunger; struggles to reflect this in improvisation and dance. Many, many struggles, but it is out of struggle that Israel, both in Biblical times and today, has been born.

And God is central to Israel, then and now.

Jews, Christians and yes, Muslims must wrestle with this.

God grant we may yet do so together, before it is too late. God grant we may allow the Father's love to bring us to our senses.

GUNS OF PEACE

A part of me
A world so full of wonder
Out of my heart
I poured My love for you
In earth and sky
In sun and rain and thunder
A part of me
I gave My world to you

I washed with tears
The earth on which you trample
A song of love
That turned your pain to joy
Look at you now
So blind to My example
My lovely world
You're rushing to destroy

The walls of fear
Which kill the hope of nations
The scream of death
Which pierces through the womb
How can you hear
The voice of your salvation
With empty hearts
Yet say you have no room?

With fists of iron
And eyes which show no mercy
You hold in chains
The life I freely gave
My children starve
While you grow fat on plenty
And open wounds
And ever open graves

In silent pain
The guns of peace are raging
What have you done
To turn My love to this?
I ask you now
To cease the war you're waging
And spread My love
Wherever life exists

I ask you now
To cease the war you're waging
And offer love
Wherever life exists

Phil's lyric *Guns of Peace* expresses the whole Bergen-Belsen experience. It also speaks to our own time very clearly. I realised that as recently as July 1989, when we made a major tour of *ALPHA AND OMEGA* through East Germany, Czechoslovakia and Hungary, countries which were even then beginning to hit the headlines of the world. Just two months later, the very church we sang in, the Gethsemane Church in East Berlin, was to become a symbol of peaceful protest and a cry for freedom of a whole people. ''The walls of fear which kill the hope of nations'' — we sang these very words within a quarter of a mile of the Berlin Wall, which was soon to come tumbling down.

Gethsemane Church, East Berlin, October 1989
© Popperfoto, used with permission.

A letter written to me by a young member of our East
German choir after her first ever visit to West Berlin in
September 1989, when the Wall was breached, powerfully
expresses the mood of a whole people who flooded to
freedom after 40 years.

> In the night we started a "wall trip". We went
> from checkpoint to checkpoint catching the
> atmosphere. The whole city was celebrating .....
> And just in that moment we thought of you and
> your words — "we live in the most urgent days
> of history." Suddenly all things changed ..... We
> met in the cathedral and after a prayer time
> thousands of people went through the streets
> with candles in the hands ..... It was an
> important event, but I hope we won't stop
> here .....

Guns of Peace makes an impact wherever it is performed.
Many people see it as the focal point in *ALPHA AND
OMEGA*. It speaks right to the heart of so many
contemporary issues, and I think it does this precisely
because Phil allowed himself to hear what I had heard in
Bergen-Belsen: "the silent pain" of "the guns of peace", and
this opened him up to the pain of the earth — the tears of all
victims of the misuse of power: the starving, the abused, the
oppressed of all the earth. Perhaps it took the tears of
thousands of Jewish children to open our ears to the crying
of our world. Once we have heard that crying there is just
simply nothing to say. Nothing even to pray. Yet as a
composer I believe that this is when music may begin. Music
which tries to convey what words can never say. Music and
movement: dance, shadow, light. But first of all comes the
silence which admits only one thing: brokenness. We cannot
begin to understand. Even the concept of God becomes
terrible. And then we see that God trembles too. We feel His
pain. And out of that pain, love. Nothing else. And so even
when my music is joyful, it is music which knows how to
weep.

*   *   *

The circumstances surrounding the recording of *ALPHA AND OMEGA* were unforgettable and probably unrepeatable! It was recorded in five different locations — three studios, one church (All Souls, Langham Place, London), and the bulk of the work at "home sweet home". Modern technology enables you to assemble a studio under the most unlikely conditions, in my case the front room of our Edwardian semi-detached in Headingley, Leeds.

It seemed entirely appropriate to allow this vital stage in the birth of the work to take place in such a sympathetic atmosphere and environment — in this case with family and friends close by, rather than overlooking a lake, in the middle of woodland or by the sea!

Over a period of a couple of days, under the direction of co-producer, engineer and guitarist Neil Costello, we brought in all the necessary elements of a 24-track recording studio — the tape machine, mixing console, amplifiers, monitors, microphones and several hundred feet of leads, power cables and the like.

Then came Dave Bainbridge, also co-producer and joint arranger, to assemble his various keyboards alongside mine. Before long the room looked like an extremely small but very expensive music shop.

There was just enough room to keep the sofa in place to provide a few square feet of sitting space for those not actually involved. Apart from occasional friends and interested parties, this meant mainly Sue and the children, Jamie, Ryan and Carla. Anyone with a young family can appreciate the disruption to the home for a whole month, but Sue coped with it all. In spite of times when the pressure looked likely to cause a volcanic eruption, our memories are very precious. The children became involved in a way that would normally have been impossible, and like no other project of mine the whole family were a part of every stage in its development.

Amazingly the neighbours heard nothing — even Neil's passionate lead-guitar work didn't bring a face to any window or a knock at the back door! They clearly don't build houses today like the Edwardians did.

But we recorded most of the solo vocals in our guest room, two floors up at the top of the house. If you listen very carefully you just might hear the sound of a Leeds City bus somewhere in the track!

There were many other highlights in the making of the album — memories that will always make this recording an unusually personal experience. Unusual because so often different parts of the recording process have to be placed in the hands of strangers — experts and professionals who naturally play an integral role in the making of an album, but who may well have little interest in these particular songs.

The choir and the choral arrangements were placed in the very capable hands of Noel Tredinnick, BBC arranger and musical director at All Souls, Langham Place. He too spoke warmly of the impact the music and words made on him personally. It must be gratifying for him to know that his choir arrangements have now been sung by literally thousands of singers representing more than fifteen different countries.

I first heard the beautiful choral harmonies of songs like *Lord Have Mercy* and *And In That Day* in a London studio called The Chocolate Factory, where we recorded the choir. To some of these we later added the assembled congregation of All Souls, to add something of the intimacy and warmth congregational singing can bring.

Finally, just in time for the world première in Jerusalem, the recording and mixing was complete and *ALPHA AND OMEGA* was born.

*   *   *

What a fulfilment of a dream to first perform this work in Jerusalem. Jerusalem, whose history bears witness to the story of the Jewish people: centuries of exile, culminating in virtual extinction. And now, in our own days, a return, a rebuilding. And yet strife and war, tension and bloodshed, all the fraught trouble our papers are always full of.

Yerushalayim. The very name means "city of peace".

Had not King David the shepherd-singer loved this city? Had not Jesus wept over it? And was it not the source of

Soldier and rabbi at Wailing Wall
© *Joyce Daniels*, permission applied for.

some of the loveliest poetry, some of the tenderest prophecy
of all time?

> *The love of the princely daughter of Zion*
> *Has been most sweet and pleasant to me .....*
> *For I have long loved you with a love that has bound us*
> *Nurtured the soul and encouraged the heart.*
> *And I say to the prophets, "Have you seen how this maiden*
> *Though battered by storms stayed true to her friend?"*

> *And they answer, "This love is a wonder surpassing,*
> *A wonder surpassing all love."*

> *And until your time comes I shall shield and protect you*
> *From those who would seek betrayal to bring.*
> *By my life I shall never fail you nor leave you*
> *And my words they are never in vain.*

As yet I did not know this lovely Jewish poem which I
would set to music in 1987, and include in *SONG OF AN
EXILE*.

But I knew from the Old Testament prophets whose words
were thrilling me with new meaning that God's promise to
His people is one of love: constant, tender, faithful, fatherly
love. When Phil and I had met Clifford Hill to talk about this
new work, we all knew for sure it would focus on the
broken heart of God known by the Old Testament prophets,
and especially Isaiah and Jeremiah, as well as on passages
from the New Testament.

After Bergen-Belsen this had to be the route. And that's
why Jerusalem simply had to be the venue for the conference
at which the work would be performed. And so, of course, I
had to go to Jerusalem. I had to meet members of the
Christian community there who would do so much to host
and organise the conference, who would be vital to the
première of *ALPHA AND OMEGA*, and who would become
true friends.

They were to give *ALPHA AND OMEGA* their
wholehearted support. Many seemed to be saying, "Here's

something we can get behind, something we can truly identify with, something which reflects what we most deeply feel, Christian to the core, Jewish in its underlying feeling. This is for us.''

This contact with Jewish Christians was to be immensely enriching for me. It was a real landmark on my personal pilgrimage. In Jerusalem too I would quite unexpectedly find the thread which would lead to *SONG OF AN EXILE* — and beyond.

Jerusalem from the Mount of Olives
© *Noël Halsey*

I had never wanted to go to Israel simply to tour the holy places. So many people ask: "Surely you've been to the Holy Land, seen all the sites of the Gospel story?" Especially after recording my own version of the Passion story. But no. That seems to me too much like a visit to a museum. I'm concerned with what is alive and real. I want to see the Israel of today. And now, having written *ALPHA AND OMEGA*, I felt a new sense of responsibility. I wanted to learn, listen, understand. Uppermost in my mind was the knowledge that I would visit Yad Vashem, the Jewish memorial to the Holocaust. I was sure that visit would be the climax of my stay.

Even at Heathrow I felt like a pilgrim, and that experience increased as I boarded the aircraft. For I was surrounded by praying people. At several points during our flight Orthodox Jews on board got up and moved to the back of the plane where there was space for them to pray, facing towards Jerusalem. So there, on board a modern aircraft, I witnessed the living reality of a five-thousand-year-old faith. I was very moved. I knew I was in touch with something both ancient and new, which had sustained the Jewish people in every nation of the world.

Our arrival was something quite unforgettable. As we touched down at Ben Gurion airport people broke into spontaneous applause. Clapping resounded through the plane: the joy of a nation returning home. "The joy of the Lord is my strength," I remembered. Such joy must have been on the face of Jesus Himself as He rode the donkey through the gates of Jerusalem. It is a joy shared by people all over the world who make their way here to build new lives for themselves in Israel, not least those hundreds of thousands of Soviet Jews now making *aliyah*, the right of every Jewish person to return and settle in Israel. Many see this as the most remarkable exodus since Bible times.

Soon I would be walking round the walls of the Old City with one of the best informed guides I could hope for, Batya, who had made *aliyah* from the United States. She had a flat in the Old City. She knew all the Jewish and Arab market people, and with her help I bought some fine pieces of carving made from the beautiful wood of the olive tree, so plentiful in Israel.

Batya, her head covered with a scarf in deference to
Semitic custom, showed me around a city five thousand
years old, more times destroyed and rebuilt than any other. I
was experiencing, seeing, smelling the reality that is
Jerusalem: the home of people of so many different
nationalities, languages, faiths who call this place their own.

Batya was only one of many people who helped and
befriended me. Among them were Pam and Shmuel, Jewish
Christians who invited me to their home my first Friday
evening.

Shmuel is tall, with a reddish beard. His wife Pam is an
artist who had been commissioned to do staging and art
design for the conference. I've never forgotten my first
moments in their home. It was a special place to be,
particularly on *Shabbat*. Pam lit candles. We ate unleavened
bread, surrounded by works of art. I recall beautiful,
passionate figures, prophets in positions of prayer, designs of
the seven-branched candlestick, the *menorah*, linked with an
olive tree. We talked about Gethsemane — the olive trees
which grow there today may well have been in that selfsame
garden when Jesus prayed. Later we were to use Pam's
intertwined branches and trunks on our programmes for the
première of *ALPHA AND OMEGA*. I took a tape recording of
the work and during the evening we played a few tracks. I
could tell they were interested. But when I went back later I
knew at once that something had happened in my new
friends. There was an intimacy now. It hadn't come from
anything we'd said, just from their listening to my music.

This time Shmuel took me out for a drive which helped me
get some sort of perspective on the lie of the land. I
remember how astonished I was to discover that Bethlehem
is only eight kilometres from Jerusalem. Pam and Shmuel
laughed at my surprise and we sat down and listened to
ALPHA AND OMEGA again.

"How did it come about?" they wondered, and Pam
added, "That first instrumental piece, Adrian, which vibrates
with the sound of gunfire, you haven't a title for it?"

"No, I envisage this work as a kind of contemporary
oratorio," I explained. "This first piece sets the scene. I'd
love a title for it. I feel there's something there, but I can't
find a name."

I then described in full that experience in Bergen-Belsen which had led to this music, and Pam listened intently. "I'll tell you what you've written," she told me. "A *Kaddish*."

I didn't understand her. I wasn't familiar with the term *Kaddish*, which has since become so important to me.

"*Kaddish* is a prayer," Pam explained. "It praises God the Creator and at the same time it mourns the dead. Among Jews it is customary for *Kaddish* to be said when someone dies. In the camps, with thousands being murdered every day, many people had no friends or relatives left to honour their memory. You have written something wonderful for Jewish people: you have sung *Kaddish*, a *Kaddish* for Bergen-Belsen."

This seemed to sum up exactly what I wanted that opening melody to express, but it was such a new idea for me that I needed time to think it through. However, not long after my return from Jerusalem, Pam sent me a cutting from *The Jerusalem Post* which described the visit of the Israeli Prime Minister, Shimon Peres, to Bergen-Belsen to honour the dead and say his own *Kaddish*.

> Amid falling snow and faint sounds of cannon fire, Prime Minister Peres prayed silently yesterday for the millions of Jews who died here and at other concentration camps during World War II.

The report continued:

> Choked by emotion and with tears in his eyes, Peres paid his tribute to the memory of the death-camp victims. But nearby Nato shooting practice disturbed the solemn ceremony.
>
> "This is a terrible place," Peres told reporters. "There are screams of horror on every side. I pray for the memory of the millions and also for peace."
>
> (Wladimir Struminski in *The Jerusalem Post*, April 1986, reproduced by permission)

This report brought back vivid memories of my own experience: the gunfire, together with Prime Minister Peres' tears of emotion, his impression of horror and his prayer for peace, so exactly expressed the way I had felt just one year before; and the very fact that Shimon Peres had responded to this place by saying *Kaddish* simply confirmed to me that this is indeed what I wanted my music to be. In fact, I sent Mr Peres a recording of *ALPHA AND OMEGA* with its opening *Kaddish for Bergen-Belsen* and he was courteous enough to reply:

> We, here in Israel, are reassured in the knowledge that we have such friends as yourself in the world, who are so deeply committed to our people.
>
> We thank you for your good wishes, and your prayers for peace.
>
> (Peres' letter, July 23rd 1987)

Not long after this I came across the word *Kaddish* again in another newspaper article, and what I read there simply confirmed for me how right Pam had been to give that opening music this title, so filled with new meaning now. The writer of the article, Ephraim Gastwirth, explains:

> There are three distinct concepts in the Kaddish: It is firstly, that in the midst of death, there is life and hope. "You have raised my soul from the nether world, you have given me life from those who descend to the pit" (Psalm 30). A hymn of thanksgiving that we can live and declare the greatness of God.
>
> It is also an acceptance of God's will. Not our will shall prevail when life draws to its close, but Thy will. We accept His will and submit to the ruler of the universe. Thirdly it is a prayer for the future of mankind, for the fulfilment of the prophecies of the unity of man in the worship of God. "May he who makes peace in his exalted places, make peace upon us and upon all

Israel,'' the Kaddish concludes.

> (Rabbi Ephraim Gastwirth, Chaplain to
> Manchester Jewish Homes for the Aged,
> quoted *The Times* April 12, 1986,
> reproduced by permission)

These three facets: thankfulness, submission and hope in God's plans for our future totally sum up what my concept work *ALPHA AND OMEGA* is about. I understood why my friends had told me: ''You have written a *Kaddish*.''

So I'm grateful to Pam for providing my title. But I owe something even more important to Pam and Shmuel: a friendship. We went to a film, *White Knights*. As we came out, they bumped into someone they knew. ''Adrian,'' they said, ''there's Richard Frieden. He's an incredible dancer. You have to get him involved in *ALPHA AND OMEGA*.''

I looked across at Richard. I could tell at once that he was a dancer, lithe and athletic. Pam introduced us: ''Adrian, this is Richard Frieden.'' At that point I was standing with my back to Pam saying hello to Richard, and unknown to me, she was mouthing a message to him, ''Take this seriously, Richard — you've got to be part of this!'' In fact, Richard danced in the first performance, with Randall Bane and Mikhail Murmane. Later I invited Richard to be part of the touring presentation of *ALPHA AND OMEGA*, so for a short time he came to live in England, and became one of my closest friends.

We found we shared a real understanding of each other's conflicts. Together we thrashed out difficult questions relating to faith and art, and how to apply these discoveries to our work and lives. We shared the difficulties of being so often on the road. In addition, I deeply appreciated Richard's Jewish heritage. He never fails to remind me of King David whose faith was empowered with passion. He enriched my understanding of who God is: King, Lord, Friend — all the things I attribute to David, who was also a dancer, poet and musician as well as a man who worshipped with deep reverence. In other words Richard opened me up to the Jewish perspective on life and faith and showed me what it

means to be a Jewish believer in Christ — all the richness of
that colourful and traditional upbringing, which in his case
he has completed with an experience of Christ.

We toured in France and Spain as well as England, and
Richard's insights, the talks we shared, acted in no small
way as a catalyst in the writing of *SONG OF AN EXILE*.
More than anyone else, Richard helped me understand the
processes of history which led me to the conclusion that the
treatment of the Jewish people by the Christian church for
centuries is not only utterly insulting to them, but is also an
immense impoverishment for us.

I came to see how deeply we have lost out in our neglect
of prayers, festivals, and fasts which Jesus Himself
honoured. Christians, who follow a Jewish Christ, have
denied rights of citizenship to their brothers and sisters of
the Book. We forced them to wear distinctive clothing, to live
in sealed-off parts of our cities, until in the end an ancient
and honourable way of life was almost totally obliterated.

KADDISH FOR BERGEN-BELSEN

The following prayer by Pope John XXIII not only gives me food for thought. It also, in a very real sense, forms part of the background to *SONG OF AN EXILE*:

> We realize now that many, many centuries of blindness have dimmed our eyes, so that we no longer see the beauty of Thy Chosen People and no longer recognize in their faces the features of our first-born brother. We realize that our brows are branded with the mark of Cain. Centuries long has Abel lain in blood and tears, because we had forgotten Thy love. Forgive us the curse which we unjustly laid on the name of the Jews. Forgive us that, with our curse, we crucified Thee a second time.

When we pray those words we enter deeply into the challenge expressed in the lyric *Guns of Peace*:

> *I ask you now*
> *To cease the war you're waging*
> *And offer love*
> *Wherever life exists.*

SONG OF AN EXILE **in Dorking, 1989.**
Nico Benus, used with permission.

Chapter Three

The whirling sword

Go into exile! Go! The wrath of God
Pours forth a mighty flood — you dare not stay —
Then flee, escape the fury of the rod,
The whirling sword behind you points the way.

These words come from the poem *Shir Golah* (*The Song of an Exile*). This gave me the title for the new concept work which grew out of my visit to Jerusalem. I used it to open the work because the poet, Menahem Dolitzki, so well describes the centuries of oppression which became the lot of Jewish people once Roman armies destroyed Jerusalem in AD 70.

So now, in January 1986, in the city to which exiles had returned, I was opening myself to this history. I was beginning to understand that the active discrimination against the Jews by Christians, which led ultimately to the gas chambers, raises the enormous question which Jewish people wrestle with today, but which Christians barely consider: "Where was God in Auschwitz?" This is perhaps the most important question of our century because it sums up the whole problem of innocent suffering, the seeming victory of evil over good, the apparent absence of God.

It's too easy to say — what does this have to do with me? Of course I don't have easy answers to these vast questions. All I know is that I am involved both as a human being and more personally and specifically because I am a Christian, and my faith therefore has Jewish roots. And after writing *Kaddish for Bergen-Belsen* I was beginning to realise that my music must express this involvement — the sorrow, the shame and the hope.

It was certainly with a readiness to bear responsibility that I visited the place in Jerusalem which most deeply exposes visitors to the horror of the Holocaust, Yad Vashem.

I went by bus, an ordinary single-decker, taking shoppers, mums and toddlers, grannies and school kids out and about on their everyday business. I asked where to get off for Yad Vashem. Everyone knew. I spoke in English, and I was understood.

That's another amazing thing about Jerusalem. It's a city of the world, cosmopolitan in the truest sense.

Yad Vashem covers a large area. After I stepped off the bus I made my way towards the Avenue of the Righteous Gentiles. Those who have stood by Jewish people in times of great need are honoured here in a beautiful gesture of reconciliation: a tree is dedicated to each person. There's a powerful metal sculpture of the Holocaust in which bodies are literally intertwined into barbed wire. And then there's the museum itself, whose documents, photographs and other objects bear witness to the suffering of an entire nation. (The literal translation of the words "Yad Vashem" is "a hand and a name", meaning "a memorial". It is taken from Isaiah 56:5.)

The crematorium furnaces of Majdanek
© Yad Vashem, Jerusalem, used with permission.

I noticed that a group of schoolboys was being shown round. "The blight, the bitter road" of their parents and grandparents, of those who had never been allowed to grow up to reach their full potential, was being made known to them.

One or two of these boys were talking together, seemingly not experiencing this with the intensity I was. That was fair enough, I thought. Many children find museums quite boring. Theirs is the business of living. But some young faces, I noted, were quiet and serious.

Then I started on my journey through a full documentation of the Holocaust. Pamphlets showing the rise of anti-Semitism in Germany, long before Hitler's "Final Solution", gave me an overview of a whole tragic history as I moved through the museum. I was devastated, but I felt that I'd gone the next step on the road which had started among the graves of Bergen-Belsen.

There were identification cards in many different European languages: German, French, Czech, Polish, to name just a few. There were whole lists of people's names, each one accompanied by the six-pointed star which is now the national flag of Israel, but which was then a brand mark, even finally a death warrant. And there was the Jewish response: newspapers from the early years of Hitler's Germany declared: "Wear the yellow badge with pride. Say 'yes' to our Judaism."

Racist slogans documented in Yad Vashem became a terrible reality. Photographs told me a silent story: old men were forcibly shaved; professors scrubbed pavements; a small boy was caught by the camera in the act of being arrested. Cameras also recorded the overcrowded cattle trucks which brought people in their thousands to the death camps where in the end, beside empty ovens, were simply mounds of human bones.

Every face was stamped with bewilderment. Silent forms were caught in a nightmare which ended only in death — and a silent world did nothing to intervene.

I moved on to the art museum and I was struck by the immense power of painting which reached the heart of utter desolation even more accurately than the photographs had done. I bought a book with copies of paintings I saw around me in the museum. Now I had something tangible to take back with me. But I should like to go back again, to refresh my memory, to keep alive in my consciousness the six million people, almost a third of whom were children, who were swept away in a storm of racial hatred. I pray that I

Hungry children in the Warsaw Ghetto
© Yad Vashem, Jerusalem, used with permission.

may return often. I pray that many, many people will visit
Yad Vashem.

The children's museum strengthened this feeling. In its
way it is even more heartrending: little paintings, childish
pictures, flowers and butterflies. Some children tried to
forget the harsh grey world of the ghettos. They used bold
bright colours and painted home; walks in the park in the
days before parks were closed to Jews; mother; flowers; a
nice house; trees. Others tried to paint what they saw:
barbed wire, soldiers with guns, the sick being carried away
on stretchers, even gallows and ropes. There were no bright
colours here. These child-artists portrayed their nightmare
world in grey and black. And here amongst the paintings
were poems depicting the same world, and one in particular,
Fear, which moved me so much that I felt sure I would set it
to music one day.

From the children's museum I walked into the Hall of
Remembrance. It is a bare place, a place of silence, an
unforgettable place. There is nothing there except stones.
And on each stone the name of a death camp and the
numbers who perished there. That's all: figures and names.
Like Bergen-Belsen all over again. Too many figures. Too
many names. A litany of sorrow.

Sobibor. Majdanek. Chmelno. Babi Yar. Belzec. Treblinka.
Poniatow. Auschwitz. Birkenau. Ravensbruck. Dachau.
Bergen-Belsen. Buchenwald .....

When I left the place of remembrance I wept. I wept
because of the terrible price the Jews have had to pay simply
for being Jewish. I wept for the Holocaust. For the children
— above all, I think, for the children. And I have never
regretted those tears. Deep within me there was gladness
that my pilgrimage was taking exactly this route: one which I
could not have foreseen, nor even specially chosen.

We ended the last chapter with a prayer of repentance. I
should like to finish this meditation on Yad Vashem with
words which I have often pondered very deeply.

> Israel's faith was put to the greatest test in all its
> tragic history, with Hitler's deliberately planned

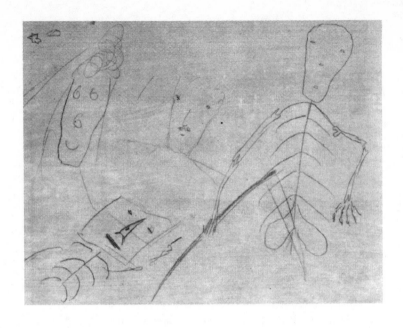

Children's drawings from Terezín
Vladimír Flusser (12.3.1931 – 6.9.1943, Auschwitz)
Julie Ogulárová (13.6.1933 – 6.10.1944, Auschwitz)
Used with permission of the State Jewish Museum, Prague.

murder of a third of its people ..... This evil
design found many helpers .....

But a miracle occurred. Those who had looked
into the depths of Hell, sang the praise of God,
said a prayer for mankind and set about to
create a new life of peace and justice in a new
land. Their ideals had not perished in the gas
chambers by the age of science. Their rabbis and
scholars, decimated by the powers of evil, would
renew their learning and rebuild their schools in
Israel and in other lands.

Such is the power of faith in redemption.

> (Rabbi Ephraim Gastwirth, Chaplain to
> Manchester Jewish Homes for the Aged,
> quoted *The Times*, April 12, 1986,
> reproduced by permission)

Auschwitz
Stefan Wegner © National Museum, Warsaw, used with permission.

Chapter Four

I would never choose freedom

I am the Way, I am the Truth
I am the Life, I am the Resurrection
If you come to Me with your burdens
I will give you rest.

This great promise from the gospels is sung in *ALPHA AND OMEGA*. It reflects a relationship of love and trust. My experiences in Jerusalem were teaching me about this relationship, particularly with reference to the Jewish people. *SONG OF AN EXILE* is centred upon it, and I explore it still further in my album, *FATHER*.

The world première of *ALPHA AND OMEGA* was held in Jerusalem on March 26th, 1986. My wife Sue and I left our two little boys at home and flew out with our eight-month-old baby Carla.

The performance took place in front of an audience of approximately 3,000 people. A small choir of local singers participated, together with three dancers: Randall Bane, who also directed the choreography, Richard Frieden and Mikhail Murmane.

Randall and I had worked together before, at a Christian Arts Seminar in Australia. He has since toured *ALPHA AND OMEGA* with me all over Europe. He is a very dear friend, someone I trust absolutely. In fact, there is a tremendous fatherly quality about Randall.

Randall is involved not so much with dance, more with interpretative movement. He is a remarkable man, with a story which would need a book of its own to tell. He is deeply committed to Christ, to dance and to Jerusalem, and so I asked him to be involved with the choreography of *ALPHA AND OMEGA*.

I can still recall Randall sitting at a kitchen table in Jerusalem, listening to the cassette through a personal stereo with a look of intense concentration on his face.

Only later did he confess that as he listened to the music he had absolutely no idea how to put across the central thought in his mind: the figure of Christ. He needed to find a way of weaving that figure into the music. In other words, he needed to choreograph a continuous thread from *Kaddish*, through *Messiah Mask* and on to *Guns of Peace*. And at that moment he just could not find the key to the whole interpretation.

But it came, and it was the most ambitious presentation of *ALPHA AND OMEGA* we have ever staged, with great use made of those intertwined olive trees and the *menorah* of Pam's work, to set off dance and movement. It allowed those present in the audience to witness a whole range of emotions: despair, terror, anguish, hope and joy — everything which is part of being human and being oppressed.

Later, after performances in Norway and Holland, the British première took place in London at the Odeon, Hammersmith in September 1986. I invited Clifford Hill to introduce the performance and it was deeply encouraging to remember together the events of the previous eighteen months that had led to this moment. Clifford was a lovely example of a man able to let go of something that was dear to his heart — indeed, something that he had influenced profoundly. And I had personal need of his prayer that evening. "I believe this is to be the beginning of a new confidence in you, Adrian," he said. "I pray that God will release you into the message of your own music and inspire you to say exactly what needs to be said with courage and humility."

For there is a vital balance to be found between the pouring out of the heart in sorrow over 200 million who have died in wars and as sacrifices to ideologies in this century, and the real and personal needs of the individuals that make up my audiences. For they may not yet have travelled my pilgrim way, and they will find the heart of what I want to say in my music, in the dance and in the performance they will witness.

And then we went on stage. Clifford introduced me and

ALPHA AND OMEGA, the performance began and a British audience heard the work for the first time.

The live presentations of *ALPHA AND OMEGA* led to interest in the making of a concept video of the work. Randall and I met to film it on location in Jerusalem and the desert nearby.

We went out to the Judaean hills to a Muslim shrine which marks a place where Moses is said to have set up camp. It has a very similar shape to the city of Jerusalem, with great waves of mountains behind and the Dead Sea and Judaea on either side: magnificent and quite unforgettable.

We set up generators to play the music and work the lighting. It was evening. I climbed up one of the nearby hills to get a view of the whole scene. I could still hear the music and see the lights of the generators below. Cameras were filming Randall as he danced to *Guns of Peace*, and I watched, fascinated. It was like a scene from Bible times: the dancer's expressive movements set against the impassive, enduring mountains. King David of Israel himself must have known this same scene. Perhaps he too had danced here in worship .....

Hills of Judaea
© Evangelische Omroep, used with permission.

My thoughts were interrupted by the sudden appearance of an Israeli army patrol: trucks, armoured cars, uniforms — all the tools of war. All this against a background of music, lyric and dance which cry out against violence. I had before me a visual, immediate outworking of the song.

Once again I heard the sounds of war rumble across the silent earth. I felt sorrow in those very hills which most especially speak of eternal things to the searching heart. *Yerushalayim*, the city of peace, is the centre of manoeuvres of war. I felt the sadness of that to my heart's core.

In terms of its ethnic groupings alone, Israel itself is a microcosm of the world. Among the Jews are immigrants from 102 nations. Then there is the Palestinian Arab population. There are Armenians, Circassians, Russians and hundreds of Westerners. And this city has an age-old commission to be a place of peace, a light to the nations, a refuge for foreigners.

I left those desert hills with a sense of sorrow. Indeed, it's not too much to say I felt a weight of sorrow which reminded me of the drawings of olive trees which could have witnessed Christ's anguished prayer in Gethsemane, and which we had chosen as a centrepiece for that first performance of *ALPHA AND OMEGA*, as a sign of hope which comes out of despair .....

That simple truth is so important. Too many people have a negative reaction to pain. The fact is that until we can confront pain and sorrow we simply won't begin to understand our sad world, and without this we cannot enter the joy and triumph which I have tried to express in *ALPHA AND OMEGA*.

In my concerts I sometimes say to audiences that a broken heart can be the key that releases praise. We are often afraid to be vulnerable because other people may hurt us, but when we are spiritually broken we have the absolute promise that this vulnerability is the gateway to healing and that God will redeem, rebuild and restore.

Olive trees, bowed beneath a weight of sorrow, remind us of Christ's cross. It is against this background that we are able to sing:

Oh rejoice, the Holy City comes
Oh rejoice, the new Jerusalem
Oh rejoice, be ready now
He comes to take His bride
He is Alpha and Omega, the beginning and the end.

Pam Suran's *menorah*

ALPHA AND OMEGA **with Randall Bane, Rotterdam, February 1989**
Ina Komdeur, used with permission.

Adrian in concert
Ladislav Vallach, used with permission.

As a musician and writer, until *ALPHA AND OMEGA*, I'd
never conceived of working on a project that would involve a
choir. Perhaps the rather traditional image of church choirs
had made me keep my distance from choral music. After all,
I grew up in the shadow of Canterbury Cathedral! But as the
writing of *ALPHA AND OMEGA* took shape it became clear
that some parts of the work needed the unique and powerful
texture that comes from many voices. The depth of worship
and praise in songs like *And In That Day* and *And They Shall
Prophesy* had to be given choral expression. I also needed to
contrast songs like these with the more intimate solo parts.
In fact, choirs were to become the key to our international
tours: Norwegian, Swiss, Spanish, Austrian, East German
and so on. By using singers from the different countries we
could draw on a local sense of involvement — our choirs,
who rehearsed and came to feel so very deeply part of the
work, often came from the actual town where we performed.
And they involved their families. We have had some
moving, tender stories about the way whole families have
been affected by our concerts, as you will see from the letters
later in this book.

I must say that of all the concerts I've given in Great
Britain itself the *ALPHA AND OMEGA* cathedral tour in May
1988 was the most exciting and moving.

Without doubt a cathedral gives a voice a whole new
dimension! It was even a pleasure to listen to my own as it
echoed among pillars and arches, returning to me five
seconds later!

But this tour, which took *ALPHA AND OMEGA* with its
modern music and stage effects into the heartland of the
Anglican church, was not without other problems. For one
thing, some of the hierarchy objected.

For another, as I said, I grew up in Canterbury, with
memories of boys' choirs and the pomp and ceremony of
cathedral worship. I was confirmed in the cathedral, and my
father, who was Bishop of Croydon, was consecrated there.
Although as an artist I can respond deeply to the intrinsic
beauty of a great cathedral, built for the greater glory of
God, and to the musical excellence that is always
guaranteed, all too often cathedrals can embody the very

things which make the church seem outdated and irrelevant to most of our nation. In the final analysis, the church is where Christians are — vital and visionary, not simply a historical landmark, or a guardian of English traditions and values. After all, the synagogue isn't seen in this way by Jewish people. It isn't something sacred in itself. For the Jews, religion belongs as much to the home: food and festivals, lighting candles, things in which the whole family takes part. This surely is what has helped to keep Judaism alive. And I think the home is where faith matters most, and is most to be nurtured and tested.

So this cathedral tour wasn't so easy for me.

I was able to voice some of these feelings in the course of the presentation when I was interviewed by Philip Johanson, now General Secretary of the Church Army. Playing the devil's advocate, Philip asked: "Why bring the message of *ALPHA AND OMEGA* into cathedrals?" I said something like this: "For many people in Britain today our cathedrals confirm their impression that Christianity is something of the past, that England is basically a secular country living in a post-Christian age. If anything, they're seen primarily as a tourist attraction — a relic or a museum — not a symbol of living Christianity. I believe the warnings and pleadings of the prophets Isaiah and Jeremiah to be very relevant to the church in this country today."

I suppose that wasn't very tactful, but you must remember I've spent many hours battling this out with my father who was totally loyal to his church.

And there's no doubt about it, those vast cathedrals provided a magnificent venue for *ALPHA AND OMEGA*, adding to its impact. One day perhaps we'll see the cathedrals become once again a focus for the spiritual life of the cities built around them.

Such tours have involved literally thousands of individuals all over Europe. Between March 1986 and through to the present day, *ALPHA AND OMEGA* has been performed well over a hundred times in fifteen different countries, including East Germany and Czechoslovakia: countries which in summer 1989, when we toured there, were barely beginning to experience the enormous changes which were so soon to explode into the headlines in such new and unexpected ways.

These songs have been performed in vast cathedrals and little churches, in large concert halls, not least London's Royal Albert Hall and the Cirque d'Hiver in Paris, as well as in a sports stadium in Brno, Czechoslovakia and, unforgettably, a hut in a refugee camp in Austria.

Perhaps this gives an insight into the nature of my work. I'm ready to take my music into any situation which God opens up, and follow a path which may be full of uncertainties, but which ultimately means that I can take the healing, forgiving word of God to some of the most unlikely places on earth. I guess the contrasting nature of these venues speaks for itself. We can play in the Royal Albert Hall and two days later may find ourselves in a venue seating less than 150 people, run-down and ill-equipped, with an inadequate power supply.

In the end I believe that an artist is basically a servant — offering himself wherever there are those who will listen to what he has to say. And what a privilege to have an audience, whatever the size, wherever it may be.

The core of these works is the relationship with which we began this chapter. Each one of us is called to be part of this, and in our turn, to offer healing and forgiveness. Insofar as we fail there is darkness — growing darkness.

Yet I am certain, and my music expresses this hope, that even within darkness we experience relationships which are in themselves small reflections of the Father love which is willing to suffer and die, the Mother love which shelters and nourishes .....

SONG OF AN EXILE was going to explore this very special, deeply healing relationship: that of the Jewish people and their God who stands by them at every moment of their history and loves to the very depths, to death. I was going to find my own response to this love deepening and growing.

We are living in especially urgent days. Although in this very century the enemy of God found willing hands to destroy God's people — and nearly succeeded — the nation of Israel has been reborn as a living, modern proof of God's age-old faithfulness and love.

All this is a source of much bitterness, of course. The world's three major faiths do not coexist in harmony in the City of Peace. But each of these three faiths is able to respond to the tender Jewish poem which we sing at the end of *SONG OF AN EXILE*:

> *If I were a child in arms and you were my mother*
> *then I would suckle and you would quench my thirst.*

> *If I were a shelter and you dwelt within me*
> *We would clothe ourselves with joy.*

> *If I were a servant and you were my Lord*
> *I would long to serve you.*
> *O, I would never choose freedom.*

It is in the context of this tender, nurturing, sustaining relationship that we find our inner peace, our joy and our true freedom.

SAFE IN MY EMBRACE

Chapter Five

Fear

People like me, brought up in England after the last war,
have little understanding of what our neighbours in Europe
actually went through during years which are still a recent
memory. For people who remember the war, and particularly
for audiences in Europe, the music of *Kaddish for Bergen-
Belsen*, together with the interpretative movement and the
careful use of stage lighting, is so strong emotionally that it
stirs deep memories. One man in Holland said that as soon
as he heard the opening sounds of gunfire he recalled his
wartime childhood and felt instantly involved.

For myself, I owe so much to my visit to Bergen-Belsen, to
the lessons I learned in the Holocaust memorial Yad Vashem
and to my friendship with Richard Frieden for giving me a
deep awareness of dimensions to events I might otherwise
have missed.

And that's the best way.

You can study books about Judaism and relate these to the
Bible, but friendship uncovers real dimensions — like the
depth of Richard's commitment to his parents, and the love
which he extended to mine. When my father died Richard,
who was in Jerusalem where he still lives, went to the
Western or Wailing Wall — so called because of the pleading
and chanting of Orthodox Jews who come there to pray.
Richard also prayed there, saying *Kaddish* for my father.

That mark of respect, expressed in this traditional Jewish
way, sums up for me Richard's commitment and loyalty to
our friendship and to his own roots; and as we toured
together, I saw Europe through the eyes of this dear Jewish
friend, and I began to see how tragic it is for Christianity as
a whole that we cut ourselves off from the very tradition
which gave birth to our faith. In doing so we have robbed
ourselves of so much which could have been given back to
us, could have enhanced our Christian festivals.

"The camps are surrounded by barbed wire and electric wire. It is obvious: when somebody enters a forbidden zone or a forbidden way, he will be shot."
(Himmler, January 1937)
© Yad Vashem, Jerusalem, used with permission.

So I was particularly interested when in 1987 the President of Israel, Chaim Herzog, who as a major in the British army had taken part in the liberation of the Bergen-Belsen concentration camp, returned to the camp with a group of survivors to unveil a new memorial stone and recite *Kaddish*.

There were those who opposed his going, and to them President Herzog replied,

> "I firmly believe that the moment I face a
> German guard of honour, and receive all the
> honours accorded to a head of state, with the
> raising of our flag and the playing of *Hatikva** —
> that will be the moment of victory of the victims
> of the Holocaust over its perpetrators. I sincerely
> believe, in the depth of my heart, that the six
> million will be there with me."
>
> > (From the international edition of *The
> > Jerusalem Post*, week ending 11th April
> > 1987, reproduced by permission)

President Herzog's conviction struck deep chords in me, because as I watched Richard dance *Kaddish* in the countries of Europe which had suffered so much during the war, I knew he felt the same.

I was beginning to understand that there were years in this century when hell on earth became a reality. Hell, after all, is where God is not, and where there is no light whatsoever, not even a glimmer.

This may seem too heavy, but I believe with all my heart that as we move into the new Europe we have to come to terms with the lessons of the past. And the person of faith, especially, is asked to examine the concept of a whole nation seemingly abandoned by its God.

Anyone who dances *Kaddish* must explore this for themselves in order to perform. Once you do absorb these things your understanding is enlarged; and if on the one hand your trust in God is shaken, on the other it is truly deepened.

All this happened to me as I moved towards *SONG OF AN*

---

*Hatikva is the national anthem of Israel and the word means "hope".

Child of the ghetto
Alexander Bogen © Yad Vashem, Jerusalem, used with permission.

EXILE. This album is centred around six Jewish poems and songs which express God's tender love for His people, and their trust in Him. A friend in Leeds, Dave Collins, had already introduced me to a collection of Hebrew poems in translation, and of course I was familiar with the great poetry of the Bible. But the whole thing came together in September 1987 when I went to Prague, where I came across two Jewish children's poems, one of which was *Fear*, the very poem which had so moved me in Yad Vashem. They revealed the nightmare which became a terrible reality for one and a half million children this century. And yet at the centre of this there is a heart-warming cry for life and an absolute trust in God.

These poems challenge my faith to its very roots. And that is only right for we are all part of post-Holocaust humanity. It is imperative that we should all heed its lessons. And if we experience arrows of judgement, so much the better, for we are looking at hell.

FEAR

Today the ghetto knows a different fear,
Close in its grip, Death wields an icy scythe.
An evil sickness spreads a terror in its wake,
The victims of its shadow weep and writhe.

Today a father's heartbeat tells his fright
And mothers bend their heads into their hands.
Now children choke and die with typhus here,
A bitter tax is taken from their bands.

My heart still beats inside my breast
While friends depart for other worlds.
Perhaps it's better — who can say? —
Than watching this, to die today?

No, no, my God, we want to live!
Not watch our numbers melt away.
We want to have a better world,
We want to work — we must not die!

Eva Picková, the twelve-year-old author of that poem, was transported to Auschwitz from Terezín, a ghetto outside Prague, on 18th December 1943. There she was murdered.

Already impressed by this poem when I first read it, I found its impact even stronger when I rediscovered it in Prague, a city then still bound by the shackles of Communism. By now I was feeling a strong desire to work with Jewish poetry, and here were the missing pieces of the jigsaw!

My first visit to Prague had in fact been as early as 1983. I travelled on a tourist visa with a Dutch friend, intending to visit a Baptist church in Prague and, of course in the most informal, unofficial way possible, hoping to share my vision of Christian music with them.

I was full of anticipation, that very first visit. My wife Sue had studied in Brno, and had loved her time there. Through her I had grown to have a real excitement about this beautiful country with its mountains and forests, historic castles and churches, its gentle people.

Two Czech friends, Libor and Jan, had prepared the way for me to visit the Baptist church, and in fact I walked up the aisle to great applause!

These friends have done much, during days of fear and oppression, to keep young people in their churches alive to a spirit of Christian freedom which must surely have paved the way for the peaceful revolution of November 1989.

Libor was the conductor of the Moravian Philharmonic Orchestra. He also conducted and trained the Baptist Youth Choir whose name, *Jas*, means "brightness". Jan is a pastor among the young people and his vision is to encourage them to express themselves through the language of music.

"We would like our young people to meet musicians like yourself who come from outside our situation," said Jan in his careful English.

So I sat down at the piano with antiquated sound equipment and played and sang a few solo songs. Then I played a piano solo: *Moments in Eternity*. Perhaps because there were no words, the Czech-speaking congregation of the First Baptist Church received this piece very well.

Performing to members of the First Baptist Church, Prague, Czechoslovakia, January 1983.
Leen la Rivière, Continental Sound, Holland, used with permission.

As this was back in 1983 I was aware that there might well be some sort of official surveillance. There was no sign of a police presence, but within the congregation there were several stony faces, which showed me that not everyone approved of the use of classical rock-style music in church.

But others loved it.

Libor invited me home to a splendid dinner, with chicken and other luxuries. It was clear all their resources had gone into this meal.

As I accepted the generosity and hospitality of Libor and his family, a deep longing grew within me: that I would come back and that one day, if God opened a door, we would do a full tour of Czechoslovakia.

Now, in 1987, this was actually taking place. I went solo with a Dutch team who brought all the equipment we would need for a series of solo concerts.

So I was back in Prague, where I experienced the joy of meeting old friends. I was welcomed enthusiastically by the Youth Choir — but I was aware of many of the problems in a church which was conservative and often fearful, closed in their thinking about what was permissible and what wasn't, and desperately out of touch with the young people of Prague.

I sensed that, backed by high-tech equipment, my music acted as a catalyst for them. They longed to make music like this, but the unavailability of equipment, together with the innate conservatism of the church elders, made this impossible. I had many good conversations during the tour, and sensed the frustration of young people in a country which until November 1989 was under severe repression. Rock music, even of its gentlest kind, was seen as something from the decadent West.

Even so, the Baptist church in Prague was courageous enough to invite me to come with this music.

On a day off during that tour a Czech friend took me to see the old city of Prague: a spectacular place with its fifteenth-century bridges and churches carved with statues of saints and kings, its steep pointed roofs.

Jewish cemetery, Prague, Czechoslovakia
Bart Hof, used with permission.

At my request we specifically visited the Jewish sites — a historic synagogue, a famous graveyard which includes the grave of the writer, Franz Kafka, and the Jewish Children's Museum, housing a store of paintings and poems which are a document to the children of Terezín. And there I found Eva Picková's poem, *Fear*.

As well as *Fear*, I chose *Terezín*, by Hanuš Hachenburg who died in Auschwitz when he was fifteen. I knew I now had all the poems I needed for *SONG OF AN EXILE*.

TEREZÍN

That bit of filth in dirty walls,
And all around barbed wire,
And thirty-thousand souls who sleep
Who once will wake
And once will see
Their own blood spilled.

I was once a little child,
Three years ago.
That child who longed for other worlds.
But now I am no more a child
For I have learned to hate.
I am a grown-up person now,
I have known fear.

Bloody words and a dead day then,
That's something different than bogie men!
But anyway, I'll still believe I only sleep today,

That I'll wake up, a child again, and start to laugh and play.
I'll go back to childhood sweet like a briar rose,
Like a bell which wakes us from a dream,
Like a mother with an ailing child
Loves him with aching woman's love.

How tragic, then, is youth which lives
With enemies, with gallows ropes,
How tragic, then, for children on your lap
To say: this for the good, that for the bad.

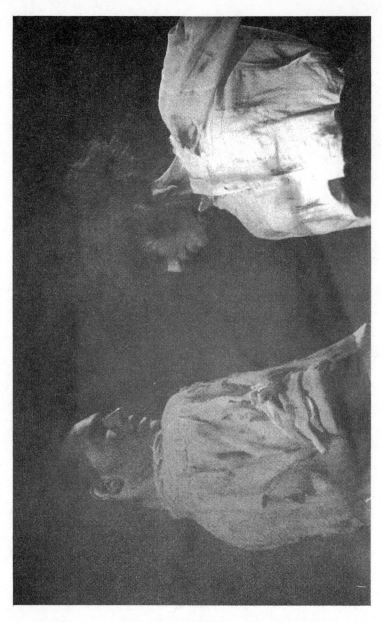

Danny Scott and Sandy Phillips in *SONG OF AN EXILE*
Joop van der Elst © Datafoto Intl., used with permission.

Somewhere, far away out there, childhood sweetly sleeps,
Along that path among the trees,
There o'er that house
And there my mother gave me birth into this world
So I could weep .....

In the flame of candles by my bed, I sleep
And once perhaps I'll understand
That I was such a little thing,
As little as this song.

These thirty-thousand souls who sleep
Among the trees will wake,
Open an eye
And because they see
A lot

They'll fall asleep again .....

Into this boy's tragic cry: "my mother gave me birth .....
so I could weep" I started to weave the rhythms and melody
of *Kaddish for Bergen-Belsen*, as well as making notes for a
total musical interpretation.

Ideas were coming thick and fast. The work would be
balanced by making the two children's poems the
centrepiece, and Eva's cry: "No, no, my God, we want to
live!" the turning point. I saw her words in the context of
the tender relationship between God and all those who are
hurt, and this is how it is danced at our performances by
Danny Scott and Sandy Phillips.

*   *   *

In every generation there are men and women who must be
heard; who speak out of darkness, and whose words,
however stark, bring light.

For me such a man is the writer Elie Wiesel, survivor of
two death camps, Nobel prize winner and a child in
Auschwitz.

Richard introduced me to him by asking a simple question,
"Have you read *Night*? No? You have to read *Night*."

He bought a copy and on my return from Prague he had it

ready to give to me, a slim paperback book in which he had
written this inscription:

> To my dear brother Adrian
>   My words can never express the darkness and
> the depth of *Night* which the words of Elie
> Wiesel try to do. It's a book which I've read
> several times, and each time it leaves me
> wordless and sobbing in tears. The night which
> is not yet over, and that which has not yet seen
> the dawn, or perhaps has seen it better than we
> are able to do.
>
> With love in Yeshua, Richard.

"I want you to read the book first, and then read the
foreword," he said.

I did as Richard asked. I read the book, that stark,
superbly written description of hell on earth experienced by a
deeply believing boy of fourteen whose mother and little
sister were swallowed up in the ovens in Hitler's evil
extermination programme, which robbed Elie Wiesel of his
faith, his homeland, and finally the father he deeply loved.

This book shook me to the core, and was a further
confirmation that I should indeed set to music poems by the
children of Terezín. And then I read the foreword by
Francois Mauriac, which moves me so much I should like to
quote it now:

> The child who tells his story here is one of
> God's elect. From the time when his conscience
> first awoke, he had lived only for God ..... Have
> we ever thought about the consequence of a
> horror that, though less apparent, less striking
> than the other outrages, is yet the worst of all to
> those of us who have faith: the death of God in
> the soul of a child who suddenly discovers
> absolute evil .....?
>   And I, who believe that God is love ..... what
> did I say to him? Did I speak to him of that

other Israeli, his brother, who may have
resembled him — the Crucified, whose Cross has
conquered the world? Did I affirm that the
stumbling block to his faith was the cornerstone
of mine, and that the conformity between the
Cross and the suffering of men was in my eyes
the key to that impenetrable mystery whereon
the faith of his childhood had perished? Zion,
however, has risen up again from the
crematories and the charnel houses. The Jewish
nation has been resurrected from among its
thousands of dead. It is through them it lives
again. We do not know the worth of one single
drop of blood, one single tear. All is grace. If the
Eternal is the Eternal the last word for each one
of us belongs to Him. This is what I should have
told this Jewish child. But I could only embrace
him, weeping.

(From Foreword to *Night*, by Elie Wiesel,
Penguin Books, 1981, reproduced by
permission)

This embrace is the heart of *SONG OF AN EXILE*. It is the
response I feel to the child in pain. Above all, it is the
response of the Father to His children in need and joy, in
hope and despair.

Portrait of Janek: Age 15
Franciszek Jazwiecki © Auschwitz Museum, permission applied for.

Chapter Six

Children of exile

I belong to a tradition that believes that the
death of a single child is a blemish on creation.
No one can ever convince me that it is possible
to kill a million Jewish children and get away
with it. No one can ever convince me that it is
possible to bring so much destruction to so many
families with impunity. I believe that something
happened to the world when it was seen what
was happening to us. Such crimes were perhaps
beyond all punishment.

The only punishment to fit that crime would
be the end of the world, and I don't want that.
None of us wants that. We remember because
we don't want the world to be punished: it is a
redemptive element that goes through our
memory. We want to save the whole world, not
only the Jewish world.

(From a speech by Elie Wiesel at the
International Scholars Conference on the
Holocaust, *Remembering for the Future*, July
1988)

I too believe that "the death of a single child is a blemish
on creation." I believe it as a father of three children. I
believe it as the child of a loving father who supported me,
whether he understood me or not. I believe it above all
because I acknowledge myself the son of a heavenly Father
whose love becomes more important to me every day.

Elie Wiesel explains that remembering the murder of a
million Jewish children is "a redemptive element that goes
through our memory." My journey has taken me to the pain
of children of the Holocaust. Soon I was to experience
something of the pain of children of exile, in Traiskirchen, a

refugee camp in Austria, which in itself is a ''blemish on creation''. Workers there, particularly those I met linked with the YMCA in whose hut I gave a concert, tried hard to bring light and hope into this desperate place. But refugee camps, those places to which people come with so few possessions and so much hope are, in and of themselves, a sign which says: ''You are not wanted. You are not yet one of us. You are an outsider, an alien. You don't belong.'' And that is why they are a blemish. They represent begrudging, even hostile attitudes.

In spite of all the recent changes which have shaken Europe, the refugee problem remains as intractable as ever. Indeed, many people have called the eighties 'the decade of refugees'. Sadly, the nineties look set to engender an ever-deepening crisis, affecting the Middle East as well.

I've performed twice at this refugee camp just outside Vienna, and both times the performances have been attended by a huge mixture of nationalities: Romanian, Bulgarian, Yugoslav, Chinese, Polish — a melting pot of humanity, troubled and confused. People have crowded here from many different backgrounds and languages. Some of them may have had mixed motives but the underlying desire which unites them all is a desire for freedom.

Queues of Trabants, Skodas and Polski Fiats sat outside this camp all weekend, crammed with a family's entire possessions, stuck for several days until the reception centre could admit them to the camp where housing blocks towered to the sky.

And when I think of that first visit to Traiskirchen in October 1987, I think of a beautiful Swiss girl who had worked in the camp for two years. She was a gentle, compassionate person who radiated care, love and sadness. The plight of the refugees, the tiredness and frustration of the authorities, the hardness of the workers who often seemed to be forced against their wishes to treat people as less than human: all this had worn her down. I'll never forget what she said — ''If I were in their situation I would take my own life. I can see no hope for them.'' The statement was all the more shocking coming from her, a woman of peace, of deep Christian faith, who brought hope into countless hopeless lives.

People pressed around us as soon as we arrived at the YMCA hut. A Romanian boy of about seventeen years of age came up to me and said in broken English: "I am so glad to meet you. Back home where I used to live one of the songs we loved to sing was your song *Only Jesus*:

> *Who's gonna mend my broken heart?*
> *Who's gonna give me a brand new start?*
> *And when the rocky road is tough*
> *Whose love's gonna be enough?*

Romania, which has experienced such historic changes, yet still with so much distrust and despair, remains one of the saddest countries in the whole Eastern bloc, and has given the West a new phrase: "Ceaucescu's children". It moved me deeply that one of my songs could mean so much to people there. I was also encouraged and challenged by the faith of that young man, who was living in such desperate circumstances.

Encounters like that mean far more than reviews in glossy magazines, just as performances in a place like this refugee camp somehow matter more than the most prestigious concert hall.

The YMCA hut is kept going by voluntary staff, many of them as dedicated as the Swiss girl I had met. If ever there was a living example of something being salt and light in a place of need, it was that hut in Traiskirchen. Kids are entertained there. All sorts of activities go on, and a large crowd turned up to hear us play.

They would put the youngsters at the front, they said, and they warned us they were likely to create a disturbance.

From the din that was going on as we were setting up, I agreed, and indeed throughout the performance they were never silent! There was a constant hubbub in what seemed like dozens of different languages. And of course there were several simultaneous translations to add to the welter of sound.

There are few countries who welcome refugees, I reflected as I looked around me at these contemporary exiles with nowhere to call home. Some children were clearly disturbed, others seemed to be coping well. But what would the future hold for them? For their parents?

So to this audience we brought the songs from *ALPHA AND OMEGA*. Neil Costello's dramatic and emotive guitar work in *Guns of Peace* arrested everyone's attention. I introduced the concert by saying that God is on the side of those who are weak, persecuted and vulnerable — one of the many truths of God which Christians and Jews hold in common. We share this idea that God reaches out to us in love and blessing, that He is our Redeemer as well as our Creator, that He made us in His own image to love Him and serve Him, and without this relationship we're like seeds lying outside the soil: full of potential but not of growth.

And so we were privileged to perform in this place where people had come because their own potential was being frustrated by repressive régimes, lack of opportunity at home. And some, indeed, had faith like the Romanian boy I'd met.

We finished the concert, packed up and left the hut. It was dark by now, very late. And there was a little boy, dark-skinned, black hair, quite on his own. No one had come to collect him.

We stowed our gear in the car, and when the last thing was finally packed away, the YMCA staff locked the hut. The little boy was still there, still on his own. He banged on that locked door with all his might, cried and sobbed and banged and battered the door again.

The picture of that child is ingrained in my memory. He represents countless millions who suffer untold misery because of the iniquity of adults. They batter doors which will never open, little outcasts in a friendless world: children of war, children who are made to feel different because of handicap or disease, children who suffer abuse, refugee children everywhere.

> *Lord have mercy*
> *On Your children*
> *Weeping and in fear*
> *For You are our God and Saviour*
> *Father in Your love draw near.*

There are at least fifteen million refugees in the world: fifteen million exiles, treading their "bitter road", with the "whirling sword" of political division cutting them off for ever from their homes.

For them too I must sing *SONG OF AN EXILE*.

"Grain For Sowing Shall Not Be Milled"
Käthe Kollwitz © Galerie St Etienne, New York, permission applied
for.

Chapter Seven

Safe in my embrace

The name "Israel" means "he struggles with God". One of the lessons of life rooted in the Bible is that so often blessing is only born out of struggle. How incredible that this nation's name should originate from a physical conflict between Jacob and God — Jacob unwilling to let go until he had received God's blessing!

In a very real way the theme of *SONG OF AN EXILE* is the age-old struggle of the Jewish people directly linked with God's eternal love. By setting the words of Jewish poets to music I opened myself artistically to this deep and historical struggle: the conflict in this relationship, the exiled longing for home.

God's answer to all of this is love — compassionate and constant.

I am your God and I will hold you
Safe in My embrace
Child you have come to Me in repentance
Now you will see My face .....

In *SONG OF AN EXILE* we perform Eva Picková's poem *Fear*. And then Sandy Phillips, who dances as Eva, runs straight into an embrace with mime artist Danny Scott as those great words from Isaiah are spoken:

"Can a mother forget the baby at her breast
and have no compassion on the child she has borne?
Though she may forget,
I will not forget you!

See, I have engraved you on the palms of my hands;
your walls are ever before me."

We used a child's painting of a butterfly to express this promise: a butterfly painted behind the grim walls of Terezín from which children were transported to die.

And now in July 1988 as we moved towards the recording of *SONG OF AN EXILE*, when layer after layer of sound would be added in the studio by the various artists involved, I needed to remind myself of that wonderful promise of God: "I have engraved you on the palms of My hands."

My father, who had always given me such close support, needed open heart surgery. Just before his operation I went to St. Albans to visit him and my mother.

Dad and I went for a walk around St Albans Abbey. We talked over many things, including the possibility of his death. There was a deep calm about him — a peace that clearly reflected all the reading, prayer and meditation he had done to prepare himself for this major operation. When we returned home I played him *Lord Have Mercy* and a recently recorded version of *Lament for Jerusalem*, with its poignant ending:

> *O that you would rend the Heavens, Lord, and come down*
> *That the mountains would tremble before you like pebbles in your*
> *hand*
> *Nations will come to your light,*
> *Kings to the brightness of your dawn,*
> *O restore us to yourself, Lord, that we may return.*

I remembered Sunday mornings in my childhood when I would hear Dad playing the piano first thing in the morning. Hymns mostly, almost always on the black keys, particularly in F sharp — a key I seem to have inherited, much to the frustration of those wishing to play the piano parts for themselves!

I grew up in a happy, secure home. My father, the son of a railway porter, went to university after the war where my mother supported him and encouraged him in his studies. They worked in East Africa for a while, until the Mau Mau troubles forced them to return home with my older sister, Julia. Then, when I and my brother Christopher had been added to the family, my father followed a strong sense of calling and was ordained in the Church of England. He had brought all his administrative gifts to the church and for a while, when we children were already students, he and Mum returned to Kenya. Dad founded a special consultancy agency called the Christian Organisations Research and Advisory Trust which provided a useful tool for the growing Kenyan church. It's still in existence, applying expertise to all aspects of the church: schools, pastoral work, finances and so on.

After that quiet visit to my parents I had to go back to Leeds to begin recording *SONG OF AN EXILE*. Dad rang from hospital. "I'm listening to your arrangement of Psalm 27. I'm fine, I'm going in for surgery later today."

He was finally operated on the next day. I was about to head off for concerts in Sweden and Norway. A phone call from Mum reassured me that the operation had been a success.

I left for Heathrow with an easy mind, but as I waited for a flight a public announcement directed me to phone the hospital at once.

"Something's gone wrong," Mum told me. "Can you come at once?"

I did, and she met me.

"Dad came through the operation all right but something went wrong afterwards. Something to do with his blood pressure. They operated immediately, and he's in intensive care now."

So Dad's phone call from hospital on the eve of his operation was the last conversation I ever had with him. He was never conscious again. He lay there wired up to every instrument imaginable. Machines one by one taking over the functions his body could no longer perform — a body fighting to hold on to life.

The nurses refused to give up hope. "It's early days ..... We've got all the equipment here. Only time will tell."

The family agreed that I should go off and do the Scandinavian dates as planned.

On my return I went straight to the hospital. And I knew Dad wasn't going to get better.

He was still unconscious but he was agitated, distressed.

It's terrible to think back on that time. I can only hold on to those words, "See, I have engraved you on the palms of My hands."

People were praying, coming in person to the hospital, believing Dad would pull through. Mum was with him day and night.

But with the lapse of time since my last visit at the start of the Scandinavian tour I could see how shrunken and exhausted his body had become.

My brother Christopher spent a great deal of time with Dad. I couldn't bear it for more than a few minutes, but Chris would be there for hours. What a powerful picture that presented to me: my younger brother had become like a father to his own father .....

The whole family participated in Dad's funeral, even our three children. We didn't want to shield them from his death. We took them to see their Grandpa in a small chapel of rest. Then we went to the funeral service. Dad had planned much of it. Christopher, who is an actor, read the lesson. We used my music, at Dad's request .....

And I remembered that walk around St Albans Abbey when my father had told me how he had overcome his fears and reconciled himself to death. Now we had that knowledge to hold on to.

When I was a child I had a thing about dead birds. Whenever I found one on my way to or from school I'd pick it up. Its stiff little body would stay among my things all day, and in the evening I'd take it home and bury it! My parents never fussed or scolded me. They just let me hold my own burial. Countless burials for dead birds which would never again fly or sing .....

Was even this perhaps an unconscious preparation for the *Kaddish* I would one day make for Bergen-Belsen, for the children of the Holocaust, for countless unnamed corpses for whom no one said a prayer?

A week after Dad's death the recording of SONG OF AN EXILE was well under way, and perhaps that particular album, with its music of loss and grieving, its promise of a healed relationship, had to be recorded then.

I have explored the whole concept of fatherhood in a later

album, *FATHER*. It has grown out of *SONG OF AN EXILE*. This whole relationship means so much to me I felt I needed to explore it further. Writing a work isn't so much about masses of original material. It's more about how you integrate themes, so that even subconsciously the listener feels the piece as a whole. The music, especially some of the piano work in *SONG OF AN EXILE*, captured my sorrow, and I included these words in the cover design:

> I will forever be grateful to my father for
> teaching me what a father's love for his child
> should be. More than anything his life pointed
> me to the very love of the Father God.

I write mainly at the keyboard and I was able to translate the "raw" piano and other keyboard sounds into original and evocative textures with the help of my long-standing friend and fine musician, Dave Bainbridge. He was the co-producer and arranger of *SONG OF AN EXILE*, and his wonderful grasp of hi-tech gives a balance to my rather down-to-earth, simpler understanding of sound. But from the start I had written some of the music with flutes and saxophones in mind. Indeed I was writing for a particular musician. I phoned my friend Dave Fitzgerald and arranged for him to come into the studio to record.

From behind the screen in the recording studio I watched him play *Roads to Zion*. He had his eyes closed. I could see how deeply he was feeling the sorrow and pain of this journey into the Holocaust. I knew how much he'd already opened himself to these events, and absorbed them. His playing said it all.

That performance was everything I had hoped for, and more. What Dave was producing couldn't have been improved upon. It was a real encouragement for me. When, as a composer, you see that your own musical ideas have caught on so deeply that another artist is inspired in his own playing — you know somehow that 'deep has called to deep', as the Psalmist wrote.

Dave sustained this emotional high through *Lament for Jerusalem*.

But then we came to the last song, *If I Were*. That piece sums up this tender relationship of total trust which is the key to *SONG OF AN EXILE*. Dave's melody on the saxophone in the instrumental opening is the foundation for the song.

And he couldn't get it right. He went on and on working at it. It was the very last thing we had to record at the end of a day when musically we had been on a mountain top!

Recording time is expensive. We had to get it done.

From behind the glass screen I could sense Dave's complete frustration. I could tell that he was becoming depressed and desperately disappointed.

"Can you mute the microphones for a moment?" I asked the engineer. Dave and I talked quietly together.

"You were inspired earlier. You're tired now."

"Yes, but this piece is too important to let it go."

I tried to reassure him. "I know time is tight, but don't worry. We can always book the studio for another day."

"That's difficult."

"I know ....."

Finally I said, "We mustn't go on struggling like this. Why don't we pray about it, have one more go, straight from the heart, and then leave it?"

So we prayed. "Lord, you know our hearts. You know what we want to communicate, what Dave wants to draw out of this music. Please bring him back to that same freshness he knew earlier. Inspire him again."

I went back behind the screen. The engineer started the 24-track tape machine. Dave picked up his saxophone — and what came out was utterly convincing, poignant, heart-rending .....

"He's made it ..... he's done it. Thank you, Lord," I rejoiced silently, listening, moved beyond words.

And when I came to sing that beautiful poem of trust, *If I Were*, I had all that amazing sound and emotion to build on, giving the words a harmonious whole, adding to the quiet joy of this final song.

Out of Dave's anguish had come music which has given *SONG OF AN EXILE* depth and beauty, colour and tone.

*   *   *

Now we had to get ready for the press launch. The publicity for this launch was going to lead me to a man with a direct and deeply painful personal connection with Terezín, and especially with Eva Picková — Rabbi Hugo Gryn.

We had come across Rabbi Hugo Gryn in our research for poems. Now Dave Bruce of Word (UK), the company sponsoring the recording, sought his help in introducing SONG OF AN EXILE to the media, and hopefully to Jewish communities.

Dave Bruce went to the West London Synagogue and spoke to Rabbi Gryn's secretary.

"May I have an appointment with the Rabbi?"

"You're in luck," she smiled. "He's over there."

So Dave went across to him. "Do you have a moment to spare?"

"Yes, a few minutes."

They sat down at the desk. Rabbi Gryn lit a cigarette. Dave Bruce explained, "I've come from Word (UK), a recording company specialising in the music of Christian artists. One of our artists, Adrian Snell, has set some Jewish poems to music."

The Rabbi put down his cigarette and looked through the publicity material Dave had brought.

"Jewish songs ..... Ah yes, I know this one, "Now take your ancient staff, O plundered Jew" ..... beautiful. Yes, and a reading from Jeremiah. Very suitable."

Then he came to Hanuš Hachenburg's *Terezín*. He sat very still. "I was in Terezín," he said.

Dave looked at him in amazement. The unspoken thought flashed across his mind. "The Rabbi — in Terezín? He would have been a child himself, a young boy. Maybe he'd known some of the children ....."

"There's another Terezín poem here," Dave pointed out. "*Fear* by Eva Picková."

And now the most amazing thing happened. Still leaving his cigarette untouched, Rabbi Hugo Gryn looked across at Dave. "Eva Picková was related to me," he said.

And in that quiet office in the West London Synagogue the boundaries of time and place melted, and Eva Picková became real to Dave too, a little girl herded into the ghetto with her family, one of whom sat before him, visibly moved, visibly involved, absorbed in the album Dave Bruce was soon to release.

"How can I help?" asked Rabbi Gryn.

"We need a venue to hold a press launch," Dave explained. "Perhaps you would allow us to use the West London synagogue."

"Of course, I'd be delighted, but it would need to go through our committee. I'll put it to them ....."

When Dave told me all this later I marvelled at the amazing coincidence, that Eva's kinsman was alive in London, but even more at this gesture of reconciliation from a Jewish Rabbi who had personally suffered the whole ordeal of anti-Semitism, and had survived Auschwitz with a deep belief in prayer and in the need to break down barriers between people.

What a privilege that he was willing to open his synagogue to a Christian singer and a Christian record company to launch their new album!

The meeting over, Dave Bruce got up to go. As they said goodbye he noticed that Rabbi Gryn's cigarette, unsmoked, had burnt all the way down and collapsed into ash.

Dave got in touch with me at once and as I heard his story I felt that here was a strand which had run right back to Bergen-Belsen, to the writing of the *Kaddish*, to my visit to Yad Vashem and the discovery of Eva's poem. I was deeply moved.

Rabbi Hugo Gryn sent Word a beautiful letter which humbled and thrilled me. I treasure it and I should like to end this chapter with some of his words:

> I have now had a chance to listen to Adrian Snell's tape and am even more enthusiastic than I was when we just had our brief conversation. The words are moving and the music is accessible and direct and creates just the right mood. I hope it will do well.
>
> ..... Familiar as I am with the story of the children of Theresienstadt*, I cannot but be deeply touched by the fact that a Christian artist

has given some of these children's poems a new opportunity to encounter a generation they could not know. It is a way in which memories can be kept alive and tribute paid to some very lovely and vulnerable spirits.

*Theresienstadt is the German name for Terezín.

In the Warsaw Ghetto
© Yad Vashem, Jerusalem, used with permission.

Chapter Eight

Song of an exile

The press launch was held in the West London Synagogue. I introduced the new album with words I want to reproduce here, because they chart our pilgrimage so far:

Why did I write SONG OF AN EXILE?
..... firstly, because the authors of these six poems belong to a people whose history and survival I believe to be a mystery and a miracle of enormous significance for our world. Significant because I believe this history to be central to our understanding of God as Creator: of God as Father who loves His people, who is faithful to them, who stands by them in every moment of tragedy and horror; of God as King who intervenes, and who will continue to intervene in world events.

Secondly, I would want to say that these poems and the many others I have researched for this album have of course made such a deep impression on me. There is an intimacy, a vulnerability about so much that is written here, that is so honest, so painful and so beautiful. I have learned so much from these words — from the Russian poet Menahem Mendel Dolitzki's *Song of an Exile* or Jeremiah's equally tragic *Lament for Jerusalem*; from the beautiful expression of God's faithfulness to His children in the anonymous poem from Yemen, *God's Beloved* or from the intimate response of love for the Father/Mother God in Israel Najara's *If I Were* — each has gone very deep in me.

But perhaps it is the two poems at the heart of the album, *Terezín* and *Fear*, that have moved me the most. Both these poems were written by children from the Terezín ghetto in Czechoslovakia, who were later taken to Auschwitz and murdered there. Hanuš Hachenburg was probably fifteen, Eva Picková twelve years old when they wrote these words. One would have to be very hardened not to be moved by the words of a child close to death in a concentration camp. But beyond that, what so captures me is the insight, the maturity mixed with the childishness of these little ones exposed to iniquity totally beyond their comprehension.

It is hard to describe my feelings when just a few weeks ago I discovered that Eva Picková was in fact a member of Rabbi Hugo Gryn's family. Somehow it all came so close to home .....

Finally, may I say this. Those here who know my previous work will know of my deep Christian faith, expressed in different ways through albums like THE PASSION, FEED THE HUNGRY HEART and ALPHA AND OMEGA. To those who may wish to ask why as a Christian I should choose to work with Jewish poetry I would want to say simply this — my faith is completely rooted in Judaism. All the writers of both Old and New Testaments were Jews, with the exception of Luke. The prophets (Isaiah, Jeremiah .....), the Psalms, particularly the psalms of David, have for so many years inspired me in my faith and in my writing. Without the Jewish people I would have no Messiah, for Jesus is of course a Jew. The early church was Jewish and without their courage and commitment how would the Gentile world have received the Christian message? And today, men like Elie Wiesel and Natan Scharansky inspire the world with their courage, their insights, their experience.

I am then deeply indebted to the Jewish people .....

Adrian and Rabbi Hugo Gryn at press launch
© Word (UK)

For myself, the great thing about the press launch was my encounter with Rabbi Hugo Gryn. Perhaps it was made even more significant because of the recent loss of my own father. It awakened a sense of potential. I should love there to be far more meetings like this, far more encounters between people whose roots lie in an identical Scripture ..... Have we ever considered how the mere fact of Auschwitz might affect the way we pray, on our own or in church? I've already shared with you Pope John XXIII's prayer of penitence. Another clergyman who has been asking these questions is Alan Ecclestone.

Some time ago my wife Sue and I watched a TV programme *In the Shadow of the Cross* (Channel 4) which dealt with Christian anti-Semitism. One of the speakers on this programme was a retired Anglican clergyman, Alan Ecclestone, who had fostered a Jewish child in his own family at the end of the war.

I watched this programme with great interest, and I contacted my friend Walter Norton for further discussion. Walter is a German Christian from a Jewish family whom I first met in Leeds at a meeting of the Anglo-Israel Friendship Society. This German man's response to *SONG OF AN EXILE* was, "Your music has wept with those who weep." As a result of our discussion of the Channel 4 programme Walter lent me his copy of Alan Ecclestone's book, *The Night Sky of the Lord*, and I should like to share the following passage with you. It raises the whole issue of how to pray in the face of the cataclysmic disaster of Auschwitz, and points to the example of Rabbi Hugo Gryn:

> We live in a post-Auschwitz world. What demands does this make on our praying? I have listened to Rabbi Gryn describe what going with his father, mother and brother to Auschwitz was like, how the millions died and the few survived, how he kept Yom Kippur in his prison camp, how, feeling he was already dead as a human being, he nonetheless prayed the liturgical prayers of his people and asked for forgiveness, crying his whole soul out and learning that God was also dying. Bearing in mind that at this moment millions of men drag out their lives in similar misery, how dare I do other than try to pray as he did? Auschwitz, said Rabbi Gryn, is about Man and his idols. It is about abominable things set up in place of God.
>
> (Alan Ecclestone, *The Night Sky of the Lord*, Darton, Longman and Todd, 1980, reproduced by permission)

*   *   *

There's so much ahead, so much to struggle for, so much to grasp, but, as our concerts and tours show, there is a constant struggle with darkness and sorrow, victory and hope. We saw this as we took *SONG OF AN EXILE* to Holland and toured again in England, as this chapter will show. Then, in 1989 we took *ALPHA AND OMEGA* through East Germany, Czechoslovakia and Hungary, on the very route which the first East German emigrants were to take only months later.

But first came the world première of *SONG OF AN EXILE*

on February 4th 1989, in London's Royal Albert Hall, followed by a special presentation of *ALPHA AND OMEGA*, with a choir of over 500 singers from several European countries.

This concert was attended by three and a half thousand people. The grandeur of the building might have been intimidating, but the presence of so many friends gave an overall impression of warmth and goodwill.

It seemed a fitting climax to three years of performing *ALPHA AND OMEGA*, and it was an amazing setting for the poems of *SONG OF AN EXILE*. Dave Bainbridge's complex keyboard arrangements, together with Dave Fitzgerald's flutes and saxophone, gave the whole performance a special dimension, and so did the dance interpretations by Danny Scott and Sandy Phillips, with Caroline Bonnet adding her beautiful voice to lend extra poignancy and tenderness to the music.

The next month we followed the London performance with the tour in Holland, travelling with musicians, dancers and a small group of singers.

Often on tour we meet people who have their own story to tell, and on that particular occasion, playing to audiences of up to two thousand people, we met an elderly lady who had hidden Jewish children from the Nazis. A group from a Reformed Synagogue came to another of our concerts, and their appreciative reaction was a great encouragement.

During that tour one of our choral group said that being on the move so much seemed to convey something of the feeling of being an exile.

I think that this is often true. Being on the move so often has its own difficulties, struggles — and even dangers.

This was clearly highlighted for us during the UK tour of *SONG OF AN EXILE* that May.

Some of our Dutch friends came at their own expense to take part in this tour. After the second concert, we had a day off and Sue and I invited them to our home in Leeds.

I was upstairs when they arrived. I heard cars pull up, but on my way down to meet them I heard this horrible bang and then there were cries of shock. I knew one of our friends had been hit.

It was Wim, the leader of the Dutch singers. He was badly injured. He had walked across the road forgetting to look to the left — and a car had struck him.

We took Wim to hospital. The others in the group sat with Sue. We were all shocked. The treat we had planned had turned so quickly into tragedy. Wim's leg was badly broken. He was off work for many months and Sue and I felt so responsible.

Three days later, still stunned at what had happened, we sang *SONG OF AN EXILE* in Liverpool's Central Hall. This concert took place very soon after the Hillsborough Stadium football disaster.

In fact, the disaster was so recent that a leaflet from a memorial service which had been held on April 30th was still lying on the floor. I have kept that leaflet with its list of 95 names, a tangible reminder of tragic loss.

I introduced *SONG OF AN EXILE* to our audience by saying how honoured I felt to be able to bring this music of sorrow and hope to a suffering, grief-stricken city. A week later I received the following letter:

> Dear Adrian,
>
> Yesterday I attended your concert *SONG OF AN EXILE* at Liverpool Central Hall. I was impressed by it and moved, especially by the poem, *Fear*.
>
> Before you started singing you told us you felt honoured to be in Liverpool because of the hurt it has suffered and is still suffering.
>
> The Hillsborough disaster indeed was horrific, even more so for me because I lost my two dear friends — they were just two ordinary fans who loved their team and would go to Timbuctoo to watch them play. To be honest, I still don't believe they're dead — it's as though they're on holiday and are due back any minute.
>
> I want to cry out to God, but I have no right. I want to understand why God allowed it to happen. But I can't.

I don't think I am questioning my faith. I
don't think I intend on giving it up or anything
like that ..... I want to answer my own questions
so that God won't be made to look the 'baddy'!
Thank you for your concert.

I thought about this letter for a long time, and then I wrote
back:

You said in your letter, "I want to cry out to
God, but I have no right." I would want to say
that the one more than any other to whom you
have the right to cry out is the Father God. He
expects it and when my own children are deeply
hurt or in pain, if they cannot come to me and
express that in their own sometimes bumbling
but always emotional way, then there is
something very wrong with our relationship.
How much more then should we be able to be
completely honest with the one who made us
and understands us better than any other .....

A letter came back:

I have cried out to God. It seemed strange at
first to be expressing myself in that way, but I
still found my respect and reverence have not
vanished. It would have been so easy for me to
have shouted and demanded an explanation, but
somehow I found it easier to cry to God
expressing my hurts. I felt so much better. I am
devastated by the disaster but through God I am
being healed .....
Please pray for me. I don't mean every day, I
just mean a short prayer when you remember.
I'd value it so much .....

Pain reaches out to pain. I have experienced that over and
over again ever since that March day when guns shattered

the silence in Bergen-Belsen. And in that reaching out, beyond the questioning and the hurt, there is an embrace, a homecoming. This certainty has led me to the music of *FATHER*, and it has been confirmed to me by all the recent events in Eastern Europe which have so radically changed the lives of so many of my Christian friends.

Sandy Phillips dances as Eva Picková in *SONG OF AN EXILE*
Joop van der Elst © Datafoto Intl., used with permission.

Chapter Nine

A meeting-place

My music is leading me more deeply into places of reconciliation. As I find deep meaning in the Jewish aspects of my Christian faith, I am drawn into an embrace of healing and acceptance.

> The Jewish people, the separated people,
> therefore the holy people, is a God-made people.
> In our nobility and in our shabbiness, in our
> cultural refinement and in our vulgarity, in our
> endurance and in our weakness, in our glory
> and in the shame of our de-humanization in
> Auschwitz — we are the people of God; a
> people not merely of believers in God — that we
> are too — but a people in whom everyone, Jew
> himself and gentile alike, meets his father in
> heaven who "will swallow up death for ever .....
> And the shame of His people will He take
> away from off all the earth" (Isaiah 25:8). We
> did not choose to be Jews, God has chosen us.
>
> (Ignaz Maybaum, *The Faith of the Jewish Diaspora*, Vision Press, 1969, permission applied for)

As we have taken *ALPHA AND OMEGA* and *SONG OF AN EXILE* to places of hurt — Liverpool, Germany, Czechoslovakia — as I have sung to leprosy sufferers in Nepal and India, and played in the refugee camp in Traiskirchen, I, and those involved with me have discovered that it is essential for us all to find a place of peace and trust and, above all, reconciliation.

I began to sense this on our 1989 Dutch tour. Then the road accident outside my house in Leeds, followed so soon by our concert in Liverpool, made us aware that danger, and even death, are never far away.

The thread which began with the sounds of war in Bergen-Belsen, which I followed through Yad Vashem to the poem of a young girl, led me, as it leads our dancers, our singers and our audiences, to the visual sign of a tender embrace, which expresses the relationship at the heart of the beautiful Jewish poem, *If I Were*:

> *If I were a child in arms and you were my mother,*
> *Then I would suckle and you would quench my thirst.*

We found poignant and highly significant expression of that embrace in July 1989 when Randall Bane and I flew to East Berlin to meet an East German choir, ImPuls, and embark on another tour of *ALPHA AND OMEGA*.

The Berlin Wall of course was still firmly in place, and the opportunity the tour gave the ImPuls choir to travel throughout their own country and even into Czechoslovakia and Hungary was a novel and deeply exciting one for each of the choir members.

Spiritually and musically disciplined, committed and highly trained, ImPuls proved to be one of the most professional choirs I have worked with on any tour, let alone an Eastern bloc visit.

During that time of emotional and social upheaval we travelled across Eastern Germany by bus and performed *ALPHA AND OMEGA* to between five and six thousand people in the German Democratic Republic.

Many members of the Christian churches in East Germany agreed that this was the most significant tour of its kind since the war.

Throughout the country the response was deep. Audiences listened earnestly and with great hunger.

Although some people found the combination of synthesisers, interpretive movement, lighting and stage-smoke hard to get used to, most of our audiences were excited and challenged by seeing the message of timeless Christian hope presented in such an up-to-date way.

In Czechoslovakia ImPuls was joined by the Czech Youth Choir, Jas. We now numbered nearly a hundred, and given the circumstances of Eastern Europe, feeding and housing such a large number of young people was an enormous undertaking.

So was integrating two very different choirs — but what a challenge too, to see young people unite across the borders of geography and language to share a growing sense of wonder and worship. All this, of course, against a background of a sad history of repression and silence, restrictions and compromise, disillusion and distrust, division and fear .....

I felt challenged to share with the choirs that Randall and myself were simply there to serve them, wanting to share our own vision of the place of music and dance in the work of the church. "We mustn't get hung up about technical brilliance," I told them. "We mustn't even take ourselves too seriously!"

One of the choir members must have taken that remark literally because in the diary of our tour one person wrote:

"More important than the music and the concerts was working with you and your nice humour!"

And someone else added: "It was great to be with you ..... and the frisbee. Keep on being such a nice boy under God's sun!"

God's sun shone on us throughout our tour. It highlighted the dark forests of Czechoslovakia as our coach spun along rutted highroads. We were saddened to see the evidence of wide-scale pollution — a beautiful landscape being eroded and destroyed by industrial misuse.

It highlighted the darkness in our own lives, as one young East German put it: "I felt the sin and darkness of my own life so strong that *Lord Have Mercy* became a turning point for me. It's great that you made it possible to go on the tour with me. It encouraged me so much."

"I felt the armour of my heart began to melt," said someone else.

Another member added, "Before we started the tour I felt very down. But during the concerts I was been gladded." The English might not be quite perfect here, but the feeling behind the words was shared by many of us during those exciting weeks.

Scene at Berlin Wall 1989
© Associated Press Photo, used with permission.

Wenceslas Square, Prague, 1989
Brian Harris © The Independent, used with permission.

Prague, November 28th 1989
© Associated Press Photo, used with permission.

We all had our different responses to the tour and the music, but for me personally the highlight was our concert in Brno where the Baptist church undertook our *ALPHA AND OMEGA* project so fearlessly that for the first time ever in Czechoslovakia this Christian work was performed in a sports hall, something totally unthinkable then, and a local paper even carried an advertisement for the concert.

Never before .....

I was to hear those words so often on that tour!

Never before, of course, means never since 1948.

Never, said the choir, since 1948 had Christians distributed posters and handbills openly and so fearlessly without being punished.

Never before had such a large audience crowded into this stadium for an event of this kind.

Never before had these two choirs got together, never before had any one of them sung in front of so many people and especially outside the walls of a church, which in 1989 was still the only place where any kind of religious activity was permitted in most countries of the Eastern bloc.

None of us could have foreseen the changes which were only months away, when the Iron Curtain would be broken down and democracy would triumph in Czechoslovakia, but even so the build-up and excitement was intense as we stood backstage knowing that the two-thousand-seater stadium was packed to capacity. We were shaken, aware of our frailty and weakness; aware too of the courage of the people in the Baptist church here who had prepared the ground so thoroughly and who had gone ahead in simple faith.

"*ALPHA AND OMEGA* is coming and we are going to make it happen," they said.

And happening it was, but Hartmut Stiegler, the East German music and youth pastor, who had brought these two choirs together, and who was seeing tonight the fruit of all his work, was tired and upset. Some problem about the stadium was worrying him.

That's what happens when you're on the road. Little things get people down. Tensions build up as tiredness grows, and Hartmut was exhausted.

I sensed his depression. I put my hand on his shoulder.

ALPHA AND OMEGA in Brno, July 1989
Bart Hof, used with permission.

Around us buzzed the noise from the audience, gathered in this sports stadium, so unusually turned into an auditorium where the great message of Isaiah and Revelation was about to be heard.

"Lord, let this place be a temple for you tonight," I prayed.

I opened my eyes. Hartmut was in tears.

"I am sorry," he said, "I can't believe I was brought so low by such a trivial matter."

But his weariness had gone. His excitement returned. He was ready to go out with his choir.

And that night it really happened. We all had the feeling we were filling a great vacuum — the hunger for spiritual things within our audience was almost tangible. They responded appreciatively to the up-to-date equipment, the music, and the words. And there, in that socialist sports stadium we were all drawn together: East German, Czech, British, Dutch, American. We knew that this special relationship is more important than any political division and is a small reflection of the embrace, the relationship which is the true centre of our lives.

*   *   *

In October 1989 we were on tour with *SONG OF AN EXILE* in Switzerland and France.

We played in the usual variety of places — from a cathedral with its soaring arches to the Casino Montreux with its restaurants, nightclubs and bars.

It was in this casino that I received a fairly unusual request. As it happened, our concert coincided with the end of a ''torch run'' which was being sponsored by Youth With A Mission all over the world. Significantly, it had started in Jerusalem. A torch was lit there, to be carried to every continent and nation as a sign that God's word, His promise of forgiveness and reconciliation, His light, will shine into every corner of the world.

At first I couldn't see how to relate this event to *SONG OF AN EXILE*, but then I saw that this torch could be a powerful symbol; and indeed it proved to be so at the end of the performance as twin brothers came quietly through the audience of about twelve hundred people, holding the very torch which had been lit in Jerusalem eighteen months before, a most potent sign that Jerusalem, the City of Peace, will again be the light of the nations.

> *And in that day Zion shall rejoice*
> *For the Word of God shall be made known*
> *As His Word flows from Jerusalem.*

That living flame in the hands of two young boys made an appropriate end to *SONG OF AN EXILE*, centred as it is around children's poems, showing us that light can shine beyond the darkness of evil and loss; and there, in the casino, we had a vivid symbol of the light of the world, which blazes in the dark.

Music is born out of that light, giving rise to a joy which could not exist without the experience of brokenness.

> *If I were a shelter and you dwelt within me*
> *We would clothe ourselves with joy.*

A little boy lights a candle in front of Gethsemane Church, East Berlin, October 1989
© Popperfoto/Reuter, used with permission.

Chapter Ten

Heart for a whole world

..... the map of the world has been redrawn .....
a new man is emerging in black, brown and
yellow skin as well as in white, the serfs of old
régimes are standing up as men, the sexes are
facing each other in wholly new ways. What is
needed is discernment of the image of God, of
the fulness of mankind which resided in Jesus
Christ, embodied in action which is of common
concern for all mankind .....

There are things that can only be seen in
darkened skies, questions only heard in the
silence of utter dismay. Such a time is ours. We
are poised at a moment in history when the
madness of mere seconds could unloose upon
the world a frenzied self-destruction such as no
generation before could have conceived.

(Alan Ecclestone, *The Night Sky of the Lord*,
Darton, Longman and Todd, 1980,
reproduced by permission)

As a musician I have to be attuned. Like every artist, I
want my work to reach out into the world. And so I have to
be sensitive to the sounds of the world I hear about me:
laughter and tears, the sound of rejoicing and the crying out
of the earth in pain, hunger and need. The heart of the
whole world is love: the love of the Father Creator who has
entrusted His world to us, as Phil Thomson's beautiful lyric
Guns of Peace so powerfully expresses:

A part of me
A world so full of wonder
Out of my heart
I poured My love for you

In earth and sky
In sun and rain and thunder
A part of me
I gave My world to you

A world which "has been redrawn", in which races mingle as never before, in which "the serfs of old régimes are standing up as men". I rejoice at these changes. Deep down I've always had this love of things outside my own culture. It's something else I owe to my father who always had an international perspective on life.

My music is European in its roots, and although like any contemporary writer and performer I am constantly influenced by the great diversity of international music and musicians that is available to us, nevertheless I value that European identity — the blend of classical and rock that has become something of my trademark.

This is increasingly the case as I work with European musicians on live or recorded projects. For example, Luca Genta from Italy was closely involved with the *FATHER* album playing beautiful cello and soprano recorder passages. In May 1990 I was involved with European musicians again on a tour of *THE PASSION* where the band was drawn from three European countries. Again, the Royal Albert Hall presentation of *ALPHA AND OMEGA* saw choirs from Norway, Ireland, Holland, Switzerland and England together on stage.

New and inspiring too is the music which results from the combination of ethnic instruments and the sounds of hi-tech. I returned from India shortly before recording began on *FATHER* and I brought along to the studio two *tabla* drums which I'd bought during the tour in a little village music shop. Stephen Boyce-Buckley, the engineer and co-producer, blended these Indian drums with the more contemporary, precise sound of a Roland drum machine. This blend became the rhythmic foundation of the opening track on *FATHER*, *Compassion*.

I'm excited too by the way in which someone like Peter Gabriel has produced marvellous, evocative sounds on his powerful soundtrack for the controversial film *The Last Temptation of Christ*. His use of traditional North African

rhythms and sounds as a backdrop moves me very much.
This music, like the scores for *Cry Freedom* and *The Mission* or
Knopfler's brilliant soundtrack for *Last Exit to Brooklyn*,
inspires me because of its technique, like painting on a huge
canvas, as well as its theme: the Passion of Christ, in the
case of Peter Gabriel; the utter despair of downtown
Brooklyn in the 1950s in the case of Knopfler.

Yes, my music is European, but what a feast of sound,
tones, rhythms, even tastes and smells awaited me on my
first visit to those faraway eastern lands of India and Nepal.

*   *   *

I was rushing around in the office when the phone rang. I
had a train to catch, but I took the call. A girl on the other
end said, "Hullo, I'm Debra from the ....." — and I didn't
catch what she said.

"Very nice to talk to you," I replied. "How can I help
you?"

"Well," she explained, "we're looking to a new
promotional campaign. We thought it would be a fascinating
and original concept to compare the hands of an able-bodied
person — in your case, a musician — and put them alongside
the hands of a leprosy patient."

I was absolutely stunned. I had this picture of those two
sets of hands but I couldn't grasp the thinking behind it.
Anyhow I realised I'd missed something and at the end of
the call I said, "Could you just tell me where you're from?"

"The Leprosy Mission."

Light dawned ..... I went for my train, and as a result of
that call, right out of the blue, I began to catch a glimpse of
what they were looking for: not the hopeless despair, rags,
bloated tummy — those awful, harrowing images we see on
our TV screens virtually every day, which cause this terrible
syndrome, "compassion fatigue".

What Debra was trying to present was much more exciting,
trying to bring something of the artistic and creative into the
reality which is leprosy.

The reality, of course, is that somebody with distorted
hands and no fingers is automatically excluded from a whole

world of creativity, which most of us don't even begin to
think about. We say, "Here's some food, a blanket ....." We
don't begin to consider the possibility of a more enriching
life than these basic needs. What about this world of
creativity? I felt, oh yes, I can say something about that —
but not at second hand. This is something I need to
experience for myself and feel from the heart.

So in November 1989 I went to Miraj near Poona in India,
and then on to Kathmandu in Nepal.

This was to be another milestone on my journey. My
exposure to Yad Vashem, my work on *SONG OF AN EXILE*,
and in particular on the children's poems, has shown me a
God who has entered into His children's sufferings. As I
have entered pain I have discovered that God is *more* to be
found in places of ugliness, of darkness.

That discovery sums up why my visit to India and Nepal
was so special to me.

Of course it was an amazing way to encounter these two
countries for the first time: to see them through the work of
a mission which draws alongside people whom we may
rightly consider the poorest of the poor, the rejected who
have such a special place in the gospel story.

It's often said that leprosy patients suffer more completely
than other people. Their sufferings are physical and
disastrous. Because this disease attacks the nerves, the result
is total loss of feeling. Burns, cuts and so on are unfelt, and
therefore often untreated. This leads to infection or gangrene,
which means that fingers, toes, and even complete limbs
have to be amputated. The psychological implications of that
are often heightened by total rejection by family and friends,
who say in effect, "Get out — you no longer belong to us."
In addition, woven into all this, there is an ingrained belief
that leprosy is God's ultimate curse, and so the sufferer feels
no worth in society's eyes, or even in the eyes of God, and
the sense of loss is total.

> *Go into exile! Go! The wrath of God*
> *Pours forth a mighty flood — you dare not stay —*
> *Then flee, escape the fury of the rod,*
> *The whirling sword behind you points the way.*

Menahem Dolitzki's powerful words might have been
written for sufferers from leprosy, who are exiles indeed.

In fact it's hard to imagine any individuals who feel less
valued than these. Christ singled out leprosy sufferers
knowing how completely broken their world had become. He
came to bring wholeness, to ''feed the hungry heart,'' and
here he had ready material, for leprosy sufferers are people
who are empty, utterly broken.

I began to realise that I was coming alongside people who,
though broken, remained dignified and possessed a quiet
gentleness — a deep humility and respect for others.

There are fifteen million sufferers from leprosy. In fact, it is
feared that as many as eleven million remain untreated —
and this is tragic because the fact is that leprosy is curable. It
brings appalling despair, but this is a world disease with a
completely hopeful scenario. And the disease isn't even
infectious, in the way we understand infection.

But out of the fifteen million I want to single out one
individual who in his extreme brokenness shows what
wholeness is. He gave voice to something which goes very
deep.

Because, let's remember, wholeness doesn't necessarily
mean rebuilding a body broken beyond repair. Those with a
mental or physical handicap whom we often pity and find
hard to relate to are surely the very people God longs to use
to bring us to a new understanding of who He is in the
midst of our own profound imperfections. Which one of us
can claim to be the model for normality by which we judge
who or what is abnormal? Society's understanding of what
has value and is acceptable is clearly not God's. We are *all*
people with deep needs — the difference between us is
simply one of degree. Instead of labelling people
''handicapped'' and seeing them as those who *need* to be
healed, we must revise our opinions and truly learn to love
God in our neighbour, no matter how different from us they
may seem to be.

> *Behold the man of sorrows*
> *Rejected and despised*
> *Bruised and broken by our sin*
> *The perfect sacrifice*

Nepalese girls we met in a village close to Anandaban
Leonard Smith, Lens Ideas, used with permission.

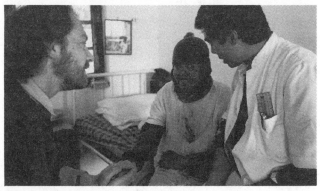

Listening to Padmahari's story
Leonard Smith, Lens Ideas, used with permission.

Getting to know a daughter of a *former* leprosy sufferer living in a colony in Miraj, India
Leonard Smith, Lens Ideas, used with permission.

See, all creation turns on Him
In anger and in scorn
No light, no beauty in His face
Twisted, crushed and torn

I found this truth exemplified in Padmahari.

Padmahari lives in Anandaban — the Leprosy Mission hospital situated in the hills above Kathmandu. The place is beautiful beyond belief. The whole region has probably more of the majesty and mystery of creation than anywhere else I have seen in the entire world. You travel over a precarious track with dizzy drops and hairpin bends. You look down across a luscious green valley surrounded by breathtaking mountain ranges. If you climb beyond the hospital a picture of utter perfection unfolds, with the Himalayas in the distance lifting their summits up towards the sky. In this setting is Anandaban, and this beautiful Nepalese name means "forest of joy".

Here there is an operating theatre and hospital wards where many different cases are dealt with; and in one of the men's wards is Padmahari. Padmahari has been in the hospital for twenty-five years. He's just over sixty now. He had been dumped at the gates of a hospital at Kathmandu. Eventually someone contacted the Leprosy Mission and he was taken up to Anandaban where he has been ever since. He was severely leprous. Treatment began at once but the disease was already very advanced. Padmahari has no fingers. His feet are distorted, his nose has been eaten away, he is diabetic and completely blind. But as you look over to his corner of the ward you see Padmahari's broken body — and his huge smile. He wears a knitted balaclava-style hat of which he's very proud. I was introduced to him and we shook hands.

In the first years at Anandaban someone had given him a Bible. I'm not sure if he was blind then, or could even read, but at any rate the Bible was read to him at his request and Padmahari came to understand that God is his father. He accepted the love of Christ with a simple and childlike trust which lights his whole life.

Over the years he has developed a role in the hospital

which is highly valued. Other patients help look after him, and his sense of humour uplifts everyone.

In all the twenty-five years of his being in the hospital his wife and children have only once come to see him.

It was lovely meeting Padmahari for himself, but then I heard a beautiful story about him which showed me how right I was in thinking that in his broken body Padmahari reflected the image of God.

Not so many years ago a father and son were admitted to Padmahari's ward. The boy was about seven. He wasn't a leprosy sufferer, but he was severely disabled from a spinal disease which left him bent double so that he couldn't walk, he could only crawl. His mother had died. His father was dying, and because there was nowhere else for him to go he was put in the same ward as his father. The little boy developed a beautiful friendship with Padmarahi, and when his own father died, this little bereaved boy climbed into Padmahari's bed which he made his home for the next six months, and together the blind broken man and the little boy made sense of life. Eventually the child was taken to another hospital where he underwent surgery which improved his condition.

There's an amazing parable here. I found in Padmahari an example of someone who is completely content. His faith is simple and real. Padmahari is not looking for a higher standard of living, his sight restored or his fingers back. In the deepest sense of the word, Padmahari is a *happy* man for he has all he needs: a satisfaction and a simplicity of faith in God which I long for.

This man, whom society and, tragically, many in the church would have written off, was indeed a lion in faith, an example for anyone who wonders where God is in the midst of suffering.

I expressed this in a poem, which I wrote as I travelled home.

PADMAHARI

The picture haunts me still:
you and he
man and child
broken bodies intertwined
fathered by the fatherless.

> *He — orphaned by disease*
> *bent like a bow stretched to fire*
> *cradled in these wounded arms*
> *head upon a heaving chest.*
> *Love such as this cares not for comfort.*
> *Here is peace — unimaginable, complete, intense*
> *nothing left to prove, nothing to impress*
> *no one to woo or win, nowhere else to go*
> *weak and foolish, poor and cast away.*
>
> *But, beloved, precious friend*
> *you have found what millions yearn to find:*
> *peace with whom and how you are,*
> *a joy in living, being, touching, tasting, seeing*
> *— touching without fingers*
> *seeing without eyes*
> *your life is like a symphony — it sings of its creator and its king.*
> *I've glimpsed you, wise and saintly one:*
> *a lion in faith, a lamb in love*
> *eternity awaits to make you whole.*

Padmahari showed me how in the wider picture everything makes sense. I saw that building the kingdom of God means active involvement in a broken world, weeping with those who weep. I caught a glimpse of what it will mean when the Messiah will one day rule over the nations in justice and peace, and the dwelling of God will be among us.

I quote these words from Revelation on the album *FATHER*:

> ''Behold, the dwelling of God is with men. He will dwell with them, and they shall be his people, and God himself will be with them; he will wipe away every tear from their eyes, and death shall be no more, neither shall there be mourning nor crying nor pain any more, for the former things have passed away.''

> (Revelation 21:3b-4 RSV)

In other words, those with mental or physical handicaps, the children of the ghettos and the Holocaust, sufferers from leprosy: the voiceless, whether born or unborn, are a measure of what society holds as sacred, a sign of how much or how little we value God's gift of life.

God has chosen the weak, the poor, the persecuted and the seemingly ugly to shame us. Does not God, who is in these, long to say to us, "You are in grave danger with your triumphalism and your arrogant and misplaced pronouncements when creation in its broken condition speaks already of the Creator!"

So the Leprosy Mission experience sums up another stage of my journey, with a practical outworking in the English concert tour, *Heart for a Whole World*, which aimed at drawing attention to this important area of need. I mentioned the phrase "compassion fatigue" already. How do you compete for attention in the midst of so many diverse areas of need in the world? And yet in the case of leprosy there is so much hope. Doctors and nurses can truly perform a healing work and see such tangible and lasting results before their eyes.

But the deeper work in me is this exposure once again to the raw nerve of pain: pain which can be redeemed and offered back to God. In that respect, as I've been sharing, each part of this journey is linked together in the most profound way and so these words which we sing in *SONG OF AN EXILE* belong here.

> *For I have long loved you with a love that has bound us*
> *Nurtured the soul and encouraged the heart .....*
>
> *And until your time comes I shall shield and protect you*
> *From those who would seek betrayal to bring.*
> *By my life I shall never fail you nor leave you*
> *And my words they are never in vain.*

The part of me that is hungry for challenge responded totally to the experience in Nepal and in India, where again I saw this vital ministry to the whole person: heart-warming attempts to bring creativity into the lives of leprosy patients. The artist in me responded too. There is a sense in which *FATHER* is an outworking musically and emotionally of some of the truths I learnt on this tour.

The timing was significant. I returned to England in December, just days before we started recording.

Chapter Eleven

Father

I dedicated the album *FATHER* to my own father:

> My father Geoffrey Stuart Snell died on the
> eighth of July 1988. Since his death there has
> been so much I have wanted to express in music
> and words — pieces that cry out to God the
> Father, words of comfort and hope, songs that
> remember, reflect and look beyond death.
>
> My father was everything I could have asked
> for in a father. For that I am eternally grateful.
> This album is, of course, dedicated to him.

In a very real sense I took my experiences from the visit to
India and Nepal into the recording studios in Bury near
Manchester. On my Leprosy Mission tour, as in my visits to
the refugee camp, Traiskirchen, I met the poorest of the
poor, the weak, the vulnerable and the ugly. This led to my
decision to begin *FATHER* with a powerful musical
statement: *Compassion*. Those profound and radical words of
Jesus, ''Blessed are the poor in spirit ..... the meek ..... the
hungry,'' are celebrated right at the start of the album and
are the key to the whole work. The album opens with a
setting of the Beatitudes. The idea of using these words, and
the beginnings of a melody had come to me in India, in the
compassionate surroundings of the Leprosy Mission hospital
at Miraj, near Poona.

Miraj is an oasis in the midst of noise and heat. You walk
through the gates into gardens which express the wonder
and wholeness of God's creation and are so lovingly tended
by the patients themselves that roses grow there —
remember, this is mid-west India! And there is a beautiful
chapel. The patients in Miraj take their own services, and
when you go inside the first thing you see is a row of

crutches and specially adapted shoes. The men sit at the
front, huddled close to musicians, some of whom are also
patients. They play *tablas* and worship God with their own
music. The women are behind, dressed in colourful saris.

I mentioned the personalised footwear offered to patients.
To me this, and the other workshops which operate under
canopies in the grounds, are a supreme example of what it
means to bring to a person something of the wholeness of
God and the compassion of Christ — not just treating people
medically, but offering an oasis in their pain, opening up
ways of expressing creativity beyond disability, so that when
patients return home to their own villages or families, they
have something to offer, something to give them value and
worth.

Leprosy is so misunderstood that many patients are not
able to go back home. Opposite the hospital is a community
of about 600 adults and children who have been treated and
cured of their leprosy, but are either too deformed, or have
been rejected and have nowhere to go. If they weren't there
I suppose they'd join the many thousands of beggars at the
side of the road. But they have formed their own
community, and the sense of togetherness is quite incredible.
The place is alive with hopefulness. There are family homes,
goats and chickens, good smells of cooking. Children play
around, giggling at strangers. They watched in fascination
the arrival of a visiting musician with his guitar, thrilled
when they could touch the instrument themselves and make
a noise.

No one feels an outcast here. Everyone has a place. These
former patients have built a small Christian chapel in their
community. It's a place which is full of joy. They asked me
to talk to them, and I told them Jesus' story of the lost son,
coming home to a loving Father:

> *Father — forgive me now*
> *I've been running — I'm turning now*
> *I've been dying — I'm living now*
> *Take me home.*

That afternoon confirmed that life is more than mere survival. There is a universal need for creative expression which is vital to us as human beings, but which is too often denied to people labelled "handicapped".

And it was here that *Compassion* was born. During my stay in Miraj I felt a deep desire to work musically with the Beatitudes. I was alone in the guest house. I unearthed a scrap of paper, drew the five lines that make a stave and jotted down a melody. I wasn't sure where it would lead, but those words were so alive in me, something had to be done. I had to voice them. There was no keyboard, but I worked it out in my head. However, when I got back home and went to the studios to record *FATHER*, this new piece seemed too incomplete for me to incorporate it into the album.

One night when the recording was still under way, I went to bed late, and awoke with the words of the Beatitudes echoing in my mind. I felt it all so strongly, but I still wasn't sure if I could risk using new material at this stage: time and resources are limited once recording starts.

However, when I got to the studio the next morning I said to Stephen Boyce-Buckley, "Steve, I want to try something which we haven't even considered. I'd like you to set up a really good string sound through the monitors, and let's just try to create something around these beautiful words."

Steve is an immensely creative person, a genius in the studio, intense, an accomplished musician. I'd seen this side of him when he was involved with Dave Bainbridge on *SONG OF AN EXILE*. He'd always be thinking far ahead, rushing from one set of controls to another, plugging things in, trying out new textures of sound. He thrilled me with his ideas. Steve likes to take risks, to try out the unusual.

We agreed to work on this new piece, and I started to play rich classical chords, with elements of the melody I'd jotted down in Miraj. Steve was excited and moved. I knew that his classical roots meant that he was identifying very closely with the way I was treating these words.

During that whole day Steve and I worked on this new piece. When I'd written the melody and the accompanying chords, Steve set up a drum computer. Then he worked out a pounding rhythmic sequence, with a hint of Asian patterns, to which I added the sounds of the *tablas* to complete the effect. ''You need to disturb people with these words,'' he said, and I agreed.

Together we worked out a solid creative expression on a piece which was until now entirely unplanned and not considered as part of the recording. I left the control room and stood on the other side of the screen, in the very place where, eighteen months earlier, during the recording of *SONG OF AN EXILE*, Dave Fitzgerald had poured out his heart on the introduction to *If I Were*. When I came to the words, ''Blessed are those who mourn,'' I thought of my father, of Padmahari, of Eva Picková, of Bergen-Belsen. It was hard to sing ..... Well, I hope the recording captured the emotion I felt.

When I finished and came back into the control room it was clear to me that Steve too was very moved. In the beautiful way which the language of music allows, Stephen and I achieved a depth of communication, and that piece became the opening of the album, the foundation for the rest of the material. It also became 'our' piece, a statement at the end of a creative day which seemed to tie so many things together. The reaction of other musicians at the studio showed me how God's word communicates across barriers of background and religious experience. It encourages and motivates, proclaims and prophesies, blesses and breaks the heart.

Music, like other forms of artistic expression, needs a sympathetic environment which leads the artist on to new forms of expression. It took an artist, Pam Suran, to open me up to all the implications of the *Kaddish*. Dancers like Richard, Randall, Sandy and Danny, in interpreting my music, lead me to new areas of expression. I have tried to highlight some moments of shared understanding between other musicians and myself. And of course, there is the response from listeners, letters which I have incorporated into this story. I'd like to share one with you now:

THE PASSION, **Holland, March 1990**
Stichting Renew, Sliedrecht, Holland, used with permission.

My boyfriend has really appreciated *FATHER*,
particularly because he has only recently been
able to accept God as a loving father, although
he has been a Christian for quite a few years.
His own father walked out of the family when
my boyfriend was just three years old and he
couldn't match his experience of an earthly
father with what he was told of his heavenly
Father.

It's really wonderful to see him resting in the
fact that, for him, God wants to fill the gap of
his earthly father too.

He has found *Hide Me in Your Shadow* to be
especially meaningful .....

Letters like these bring a deep encouragement to the artist
too.

Out of shared encouragement new music is born. After
recording *SONG OF AN EXILE* I began to feel that I wanted
to get back to my roots — and for me this meant going back
to the piano, and the acoustic sounds reminiscent of the days
when I had recorded my first album, *FIREFLAKE*, in 1975
when I was twenty-one years old and barely out of music
college.

The centrepiece in the studio for the recording of *FATHER*
became a beautiful Steinway grand piano. As I worked with
Luca Genta on cello and recorder, Gill Balmain on the cor
anglais and oboe and Julian Gregory on the violin, we built
the basis of more intimate, acoustic-sounding music,
reflecting the heart of what I wanted to bring.

I chose psalms and lyrics which look beyond death, and,
as with *SONG OF AN EXILE*, I wanted words and music to
offer a glimpse into who God is as Father.

I chose to re-record the song *Goodbye October*. Dad had
made a note, just weeks before his death, of items he wished
to be included in his own funeral service. This song was one
of them. Naturally I went back to these words with a very
different perspective. It is a reflective song which asks:

Goodbye October
Did we see the colours change?
Are we all too busy rushing through the year?

The seasons of the year counterpoint the seasons of life. I wanted this song to make a statement about my father as well as about the album as a whole. I placed it after *Compassion*, and after words I'd chosen from Ecclesiastes:

> Remember your Creator
> in the days of your youth,
> before the days of trouble come
> and the years approach when you will say,
> "I find no pleasure in them" —
> before the sun and the light
> and the moon and the stars grow dark,
> and the clouds return after the rain; .....
> and the dust returns to the ground it came from
> and the spirit returns to God who gave it.

(Ecclesiastes 12:1-2,7 NIV)

Each of the songs, each piece of music or spoken statement has its own quite specific place in the album. Musically, this work does indeed go back deep into my roots. *Goodbye October* and the instrumental *Within Me* which is played on guitar, recorder and violin had been written in essence years ago when I was staying with the Christian community at Lee Abbey in North Devon. Music is a strange, ethereal language. I didn't know when I would use this piece. I just knew it was something I felt very strongly about. Then, the August after Dad died, I was in the Lake District, walking in the Cumbrian Hills. The wind was gusting, and rain was on its way. I felt I was crying out to my lost father. I had mourned his loss to some extent during the recording of *SONG OF AN EXILE*, but in fact, I had had no real chance for quiet, no time laid aside for sorrow or reflection. So there I was in my grief, and suddenly this piece of music, written years before, came flooding back into my mind, and now its purpose and meaning were clear to me. No words were needed.

As for the lyric *Father*, I actually began to write these words on the British Airways flight home from India. The words came and I wrote some of them on the menu because I didn't have any spare paper. It was during this flight that I penned the poem about Padmahari. I was full of many mixed emotions on the journey that was taking me from Third World to First in a matter of hours.

The music had already been written and so when I got home I felt I had the essence of what I wanted to express. At the end of this piece musically I return to the same theme which runs like a thread through *Kaddish* and on into *If I Were*, forging the different albums into a whole. Each time it occurs it receives a different treatment, of course, but if you uncover the layers the basic melody continues the journey right through from *ALPHA AND OMEGA* to *FATHER*.

With music, as with any written language, you develop a growing vocabulary which becomes part of your own special way of communicating, and that is certainly what I am doing here with a chord sequence which allows for a fairly broad melodic treatment. If you are familiar with these different albums you will identify various sequences, patterns, chords, melodies, rhythms and musical ideas which are particular to me. After all, music is a very personal language.

I search for poetic images as I expose the raw nerve of experience and weave this into music. It's all one journey, a continuous quest. *They Shall Be Comforted*, written for piano and cello, flows out of the ending of *Father*. This is followed by those glorious words from Revelation, ''the dwelling of God is with men.'' And then, as an epilogue, this simple anthem of hope, *No More Tears*:

No more tears
Do you hear
There won't be any crying
Won't have to fear what dying can do
We will all be shining new

No more pain
Do you hear
There won't be any sorrow
Won't have to fear what tomorrow can do
We will all be shining ..... new

Nothing but goodness
Nothing but peace
Nothing but heaven's sweet release
Don't you know it's all coming true
One day we'll be
Shining new

This lovely lyric was written years before by Phil Thomson, and I'd set it to music. As with *Within Me* it had lain dormant. Then within the space of a few months Phil lost his mother and I my father and *No More Tears* took on a new dimension.

Some months after recording *FATHER* I toured *THE PASSION* throughout Holland. This piece had first been recorded ten years previously and was premièred with a special presentation for Easter on BBC Radio 1. A total of fifteen thousand people attended the presentations in Holland, which involved actors, singers and dancers, a large choir and a superb band.

Later in the year I went back to Holland with Sue and the children, this time to attend an annual seminar for Christian artists. One of the most valuable aspects of this seminar is its international flavour. Friendships develop among artists from very different cultural backgrounds which so often lead to enriching, fruitful working relationships.

This happened as we performed *THE PASSION* once again to an audience drawn from thirty different countries across Western and Eastern Europe. In Eastern Europe the role of religious artists is valued and accepted. And now, of course, there is a new celebration of the freedom to express faith that is reflected through the arts.

In August 1990 this was brought home to me as the family and I were privileged to move on from Holland to a similar seminar in East Berlin, the first of its kind in the territory

that was just two months away from reunification with West
Germany. It was just one year after the *ALPHA AND
OMEGA* tour there. I shall never forget the rows of empty
booths at what were once border checkpoints, a testimony to
the speed at which events had moved. Who would have
imagined on that tour with ImPuls that in such a short time
the Wall would be demolished, the Snell family would collect
pieces to take home, and I would be singing in a sports
stadium which had once hosted major Communist gatherings
where Khrushchev himself had spoken!

How exciting to be involved with my music in the early
days of new freedom of expression in countries where
Christian artists have so much to say.

Into this challenge must come, however, the whole
question of "Christian" music — its definition and role. If
Christian artists, musicians and writers operate within
"ghettos" and are increasingly marginalised by a secular
society in the West, what have we to offer churches in
Eastern Europe which are shaking off decades of oppression?
Contemporary Christian music is often shallow and
plagiaristic, lacking originality, depth and maturity. The hard
fact is that many evangelicals basically "make do". Music
and the arts generally are only valued as a tool for
evangelistic purposes, and this imposes its own censorship,
so that potentially gifted artists have to struggle with the
whole question of role as well as of talent.

So many Christians have a narrow view of what
communicates the wonder and majesty of God. The need to
label, underline and comment is a particular flaw within the
evangelical world, from which, of course, "Gospel" music or
"Christian" music originates. No wonder then that so many
within this sphere of work are undergoing something of an
identity crisis — where do I belong? How do I find a voice
which is allowed the freedom to speak without
preconditions, the freedom to draw artistic truth from the
wonder of God's creation without the need to channel the
experience into "a message"?

The arts in their richest sense are all too little a part of the life of the Church — and the consequence of neglect is starvation. Where are the young artists in colleges of music, dance, drama, art whose faith and talent are jointly being fostered so that they will be ready to become powerful and mature voices in the next generation? The reality is that often artists are like a chrysalis, tightly enclosed in a cocoon, bursting to be free, to become the butterfly, but they are muffled by an iron fist, silenced by a voice which says "No!" So the chrysalis dies, the butterfly is stillborn.

Artists are rarely encouraged to become excellent in their particular discipline. And yet true excellence touches the eternal. "A thing of beauty is a joy for ever," as Keats put it. We live in the age of the ephemeral, of "built-in obsolescence", but the artist, as Tolkien and C. S. Lewis agreed, is a "sub-creator", drawing out of eternity, perfecting his talent to the glory of God. How badly we need a renaissance, a radical rethink.

In the book I've already quoted from, *The Night Sky of the Lord*, Alan Ecclestone makes a plea for:

> a new vision of the involvement of Christianity
> with the history of mankind and a new readiness
> to use poetry, drama, dance, music and all the
> arts to express what this involvement means.

This is an enormous area facing the Church. Here, as in the whole question of Jewish Christian traditions, the arts are key tools. How profoundly enriched the Church becomes as we rediscover, celebrate and embrace our Jewish roots, and it is the same with the arts. As Alan Ecclestone points out, poetry, music, dance, painting can uniquely reach back into history and express the journey.

And as I look back over my personal journey, I see how deeply interlinked it all is, rather like the music which binds my albums together. Terezín and Traiskirchen, the Romanian refugee, Padmahari, Eva Picková are all strands of the same melody. They have drawn me into a new understanding of words expressed far, far better than any of my own, the words of Jesus as I sing them at the very beginning of the album *FATHER*:

*Blessed are the poor in spirit
for theirs is the Kingdom of heaven
Blessed are those who mourn
for they will be comforted.*

*Blessed are the meek
for they will inherit the earth
Blessed are those who hunger
and thirst for righteousness.*

*Blessed are the merciful
for they will be shown mercy
Blessed are the pure in heart
for they shall see their God*

*Blessed are the peacemakers
for they will be called sons of God
Blessed are those who are persecuted
because of righteousness
for theirs is the Kingdom of Heaven
Rejoice and be glad
for great is your reward in Heaven*

Responses and Reviews

Extracts from letters

I found [*ALPHA AND OMEGA*] really moving. Spiritually and musically, it's very powerful .....
  I do pray that God will greatly bless and use it, and continue to guide you in working for Him in this important field.
(Lord Coggan, former Archbishop of Canterbury)

A purging of long-buried pain and anguish
At the time of the concert we were going through a period of great personal crisis (and still are for that matter) ..... I can only say that *ALPHA AND OMEGA* has been the means of purging a great deal of long-buried pain and anguish. We wept through most of the concert and still do often when playing the tape, which has become almost a daily rite! .....
ALPHA AND OMEGA confirmed and strengthened our recent recognition of the true meaning of the Passion of the Cross. The hardest pain we have to bear, far worse than any physical agonies, is the pain of rejected love: the helplessness that comes from seeing people we love taking paths that will inevitably lead to their self-destruction and being unable to stop it. For me *Guns of Peace* expresses this exactly. Your songs have moved us more than words can say .....

My faith grows stronger
My husband has cancer. The hospital says that the future is very bleak ..... I listen to the tape and I know my faith grows stronger.

Takes more space inside
(From Eastern Europe): As we sing I feel how God fills me with joy and speaks to me. The message of *ALPHA AND OMEGA* takes more space inside after every concert.

Extracts from a diary kept by the singers on the 1989 Dutch tour of *SONG OF AN EXILE.*

We are not a choir yet, I can hear that ..... But during the day I realise that the singing gets better. Hooray! We dare to be ourselves now. The arrangements of *SONG OF AN EXILE* arrived. The ink is still wet. We talk about *Terezín*, written by a boy of 15 years old. It is as if a knife cuts my soul when I read those words.

It's fantastic! The sound of 100 people is great. I don't hear anyone who sings the same part as I do, so I have to get used to that.

It takes a lot of energy to handle all these impressions.

I think that this evening it was the first we (the singers) knew that *SONG OF AN EXILE* was also *our* message.

After the concert I talked with a girl who had been in Theresienstadt (Terezín). The dance and mime really spoke to her.

Monday we had a day off. I talked to people about the tour. About the reality of sorrow when you sing 'No, no, my God' and want to sing this with your heart. To think about those people crying out to their God. Children .....

SONG OF AN EXILE. Beautiful, each time more beautiful. Every time another part touched me. On one side the deep pain and on the other side the all-embracing love of God for His people.

Reviews

Uncommon scope and power
ALPHA AND OMEGA ..... is a musical of uncommon scope and power — as it would have to be, given that it is based on thundering apocalyptic texts in Isaiah and Revelation. The soundtrack is a fascinating combination of classical, folk, rock and technopop, featuring a dazzling array of synthesizers and a giant gospel choir.
(Bob Darden, *Billboard*, May 1987)

I could have wept ..... with the martyrs
I could have wept in sympathy with the martyrs of Bergen-Belsen ..... Adrian Snell's musical resources will astonish those who tend to write off the popular idiom. He is ..... accomplished on all keyboards and guitar, and is evidently willing to listen to and use a wide range of musical expression .....
(*Church Times*)

Poignant interpretation
In *SONG OF AN EXILE* the Leeds-based composer takes us into the mystery and miracle of the Jewish people by drawing on the biblical books of Lamentations and Isaiah — as well as medieval Jewish writings. But perhaps the most poignant of all are his musical interpretations of two poems written by children who died in the Auschwitz concentration camp during the Holocaust .....
(*Jewish Gazette*, Friday, 14th April, 1989)

The story of us all ..... a very special gift
The beauty of Adrian's latest work does not lie on the surface. It reveals itself as you return to listen to the words and music regularly and attentively ..... The story Adrian unfolds is not just about the Jews. It's the story of us all. Who can now doubt, as news of horrors inflicted on children in this day and age hit the headlines, that we live close to hell ourselves in the British Isles .....

SONG OF AN EXILE is a very special gift. Let's pray that many will listen and allow it time to do its work of healing and reconciliation.
(David Hotton, *Christian Music*, Summer 1989)

A compelling musical statement
On this album ..... there's a fresh accessibility to go alongside the dazzling musicianship. Exploring ..... the link between the love of our earthly and Heavenly Fathers ..... the album is a compelling and musical statement ..... In its breathtakingly beautiful moments ..... *FATHER* emanates a luminous joy which shines like a torch in a mine shaft ..... overflowing with the warm security and everlasting hope only found in the arms of the Father.
(Tony Cummings, *Cross Rhythms* No 2, July 1990)

ALPHA AND OMEGA
Kaddish For Bergen-Belsen, The Nations Rage And Fall, Nobody Listens, Messiah Mask (Pretender To My Throne), I Am Your God, Guns Of Peace, No Escape, Child Of Darkness, I Am Your God, Man Of Sorrows, I Am The Way, Lord Have Mercy, Streams In The Desert/And They Shall Prophesy, And In That Day, He Lives In You, Alpha And Omega (The Beginning And The End).
Word (UK) Ltd.   MYRCD1210, MYRC1210, MYRR1210
Song Book (MP 9517) and Study Guide (YB9178) also available.

SONG OF AN EXILE
Roads To Zion, The Song Of An Exile (Shir Golah), Lament For Jerusalem (How Deserted Lies The City), Terezín, Fear, Roads To Zion (Part Two), God's Beloved, If I Were.
Word (UK) Ltd.   MYRCD1255, MYRC1255, MYRR1255

FATHER
Compassion, Ecclesiastes 12, Goodbye October, Hide Me In Your Shadow, Out Of The Deep, Psalm 139, Your Way To Me, In Pastures Green, The Lord's My Shepherd, Carry Me In Your Heart, Psalm 131/Compassion Reprise, Within Me, Father, They Shall Be Comforted, Revelation 21, No More Tears.
Word (UK) Ltd.   MYRCD1268, MYRC1268, MYRR1268

For further information please write to:
   A.S. Management
   11 Junction Road
   Oldfield Park
   Bath
   BA2 3NQ
   United Kingdom
   Phone: 0225-483223
   Fax: 0225-483201